"I am increasingly concerned and how they crush the souls of people. I have been so fortunate to get to know Lance Witt over the last few years, and with *Your ONE Life*, Lance gets to the heart of how to care for your one and only life. This is a critically important read for every person."

Carey Nieuwhof, author, speaker, podcaster

"You are going to love this book! Not because it will help you become a better teammate, leader, spouse, parent, or friend (though it will), but instead because it will help you become a better *you*! Lance doesn't just present the principles—he gives us the practices for living a better, healthier life. I've said it out loud several times to my teammates, 'When I grow up, I want to be just like Lance Witt.' Lance has now written the manual with all his most important life hacks to help me do just that."

Tony Morgan, founder and lead strategist of The Unstuck Group; author of *The Unstuck Church*

"My good friend Lance Witt has given us a road map for living a healthy and rich life. In this book, he poignantly reminds us that we get only one shot at this gift called life. He not only reminds us that the clock is ticking, but he also provides us biblical, helpful, and practical instruction for navigating life's journeys. This book is a compelling call to self-leadership—to make sure you steward well *Your ONE Life*."

Chip Ingram, founder and CEO of Living on the Edge; author of *Yes, You Really Can Change*

"Lance Witt has done it again! His book *Your ONE Life* will challenge and inspire you to live your best life every day. Lance reminds us what matters most in life and then carefully guides us to the place where each of us can take hold of the life God has waiting for us. As personal friends, we have witnessed Lance's life up close. He not only writes about making the most of everyday but also lives it. He is an expert guide for anyone wanting to claim the full life Jesus came to give."

Todd and Julie Mullins, senior pastors at Christ Fellowship Church

"Far too often we read books from people who are great practitioners but not great practicers. I've seen up close with Lance and his wife, Connie, that he can write and speak with authority on what it means to live a *full*, *good*, and *godly* life—*Your ONE Life*! This book reminded me of some things I knew and needed to revisit, taught me some things I want to start and to stop, and showed me what it means to put flesh to what I like to call 'the good life.' If there is someone we should be listening to about what it means to really flourish spiritually, relationally, and emotionally in this one life, it's Lance Witt. Thank you for this gift, Lance!"

Brian Carpenter, founder of the Refuge Foundation

"If you feel like you are meandering through life without a clear sense of meaning, if you suspect that the speed of your life is eclipsing real significance, if you need a personal life manifesto for more intentional influence, then my friend Lance Witt has written this book for you. Lance's wisdom has added rich value to my soul. *Your ONE Life* will do the same for you."

Daniel Henderson, founder and president of Strategic Renewal; author of *Transforming Prayer*

YOUR
ONE
LIFE

YOUR
ONE
LIFE

Own It. Live It. Love It.

LANCE WITT

BakerBooks

a division of Baker Publishing Group
Grand Rapids, Michigan

Published by Baker Books
a division of Baker Publishing Group
PO Box 6287, Grand Rapids, MI 49516-6287
www.bakerbooks.com

Printed in the United States of America

Library of Congress Cataloging-in-Publication Data
Names: Witt, Lance, author.
Title: Your one life : own it. live it. love it. / Lance Witt.
Description: Grand Rapids, Michigan : Baker Books, a division of Baker Publishing
    Group, [2021] | Includes bibliographical references. |
Identifiers: LCCN 2021003701 | ISBN 9780801075698 (paperback) | ISBN
    9781540901668 (casebound) | ISBN 9781493430338 (ebook)
Subjects: LCSH: Christian life.
Classification: LCC BV4501.3 .W585 2021 | DDC 248.4—dc23
LC record available at https://lccn.loc.gov/2021003701

21   22   23   24   25   26   27   7   6   5   4   3   2   1

In dedication to
Jonathan, Ryanne,
Macy, Piper,
Meagan, Mychal John,
Emery, Willow

Just typing your names fills me with profound gratitude. Each of you, in your own unique way, has been an incredible joy and blessing to us. I love you . . . I am proud of you . . . I believe in you . . . I pray for you . . . I love spending time with you. My life is richer because of you.

Two of the titles that I wear most proudly are Dad and Pops. I am beyond grateful that we get to do life together. I treasure the moments and memories that we share as a family.

I wanted to dedicate this book to you because it contains much of what I have learned about life and want to pass on to you. My hope is that what you see in me really puts flesh on the words of these chapters. One of the deepest longings of my one and only life is to help you live a life that honors God and is deeply fulfilling.

Solomon was spot-on when he wrote,

> The father of godly children has cause for joy.
> What a pleasure to have children who are wise.
> Proverbs 23:24

One of the great joys of my life is to have a life-giving friendship with my adult kids and their spouses. You have been an incredible cause for joy. And it's such a pleasure to have children who are wise and godly.

Solomon also nailed it when he said,

> Grandchildren are the crowning glory of the aged.
> Proverbs 17:6

As a friend once told me, grandparenting is one of the few things in life that isn't overrated. He was right. The four little girls who call me Pops mean more to me than I could ever begin to express. I hope that in the years to come this book will be a source of hope and encouragement and wisdom and LIFE for you.

Contents

Part 3: It's About Time!

Part 4: Enjoying Life *with* God

Part 5: Practicing the Presence of People

Foreword

"DO YOU NEED a ride home again?"

In the life of a pastor's kid, that question is a special rite of passage—something we look back on with an odd sense of pride. As kids, we spent a fair amount of our childhood at the church. This meant a couple things: we knew where the good snacks were hidden, we knew the baptismal was a rookie hiding spot, and we knew that on occasion the Sunday school teacher, or maybe the cool co-pastor (love you, Tim!), might have to bring us home because we slipped through the cracks of Mom and Dad's communication that day.

It never bothered or concerned us. In fact, we barely even noticed. We were church kids. We felt our own sense of ownership in that place. We just understood that church work was hard . . . and there was a lot of it.

Mom never thought it was that funny, but it's easy for all of us to laugh at it now. We might have been left behind, but we always knew we weren't forgotten. And as we look back at those moments now, such situations were clearly a symptom of the hectic and hurried lives of a young, ambitious couple trying to navigate life. They lost track of us because they were distracted by the noble and worthy goal of building God's church. But in the midst of any worthwhile pursuit, it's easy to lose track of things that really matter.

Today, things are very different.

As we've grown older, it's been incredibly special to see our parents, and especially our dad, not just acknowledge that hurry and ambition are areas to pay attention to in his life but also commit himself to living the solutions and helping others do the same.

Our dad has always lived with intent—with purpose and determination. But those things are now properly focused on and correctly aimed at what is truly important.

In the last fifteen years, we've had front-row seats to his incredible and inspiring transformation. The drive and ambition are still there, but what's getting his attention and his intention are the things that matter most. His calendar is filled with family-oriented activities. He's always wanting to brainstorm how we can do more life together, make more memories. He walks slower (oh man, he used to be the fastest walker in any parking lot). He's more patient. He asks better questions . . . and listens carefully to the answers. He's more generous. He laughs more. He cries more. He plays more golf—not better golf, but more of it. He FaceTimes more. Overall, he's learned to slow down, to savor the moment.

Our dad talks openly and honestly in this book about the shortcomings of being an overly ambitious and hurried person. And because of that, one of the greatest joys in our lives has been to see him become a grandfather to his four granddaughters. He's embraced that role with a tenacity and passion that are emotional to write about. He's persistent in his pursuit of relationship with each of them and plays an active and significant role in their lives. He speaks encouragement, godly truth, wisdom, and life into them—always without hurry or a rush to get to the next thing. Whether it's one-on-one date nights with Pops or the yearly cousin camp adventures, he's creating intentional moments and memories with each of them. And to our knowledge, he hasn't left them anywhere yet.

We understand it can be difficult to trust an invisible author and give credibility to a life that is only described on the page. Our hope is that our words and our experiences can provide sufficient testimony to the incredible wisdom and insight in this book, as well as to the rich life and legacy our dad is crafting now. He has given the latter part of his professional life to helping people realize how to live their one life with intention, and we believe there are practical and applicable truths available for you as well. His desire is for you to learn from his story so you don't have to come face-to-face with the hard truths. That's the kind of person our dad is. The kind who doesn't waste his story.

We encourage you to lean into the godly wisdom present in the pages in front of you. This is the story of a life well-lived, and we believe it can provide insight and a road map to living a more rewarding, God-honoring, and fruitful life. We hope you'll take the time to apply the practical next steps and wrestle with the questions inside, as they will provide clarity and direction.

If this book had been written fifteen years ago, it would have been great, but it mostly would have been a tactical guide on how to optimize your personal performance. So read this not as a manual for personal improvement but as a letter of instruction on how to steward well the only life you will ever have. A letter filled with timely lessons from someone who genuinely understands the struggle but realized there's a better way.

We believe this book serves as a great reminder that regardless of where you find yourself today, regardless of your position in life, regardless of whether you understand your purpose, it's never too late to take the reins and change the story—to make your one life a great life.

Jonathan Witt and Meagan Maltbie

How to Get the Most Out of This Book

PEOPLE APPROACH BOOKS in a variety of ways. Some scan the pages trying to get through as much content as quickly as possible. Others highlight key sentences or sections. Some people I know always have five or six books going at one time. I have one friend who takes all the key learnings and writes them on the inside of the back cover. There is not one right way to read a book.

But I want to share with you what I believe will help you maximize your reading of this book. It is a gift that you would choose to spend your time reading *Your ONE Life*, so I wanted to give you a couple ideas that might help as you engage the content.

1. *Read slowly.* The chapters have intentionally been written so that you could read a chapter in a short amount of time. Since this is a book about the meaning and quality of your one and only life, it will be helpful to slow down a bit. At the pace of one chapter per day, you can complete the book in a month. As you read, take time to ponder and reflect. You'll be glad you did.

2. *Read with a friend.* The friend might be a co-worker, a golfing buddy, your spouse, or your small group at church.

At the end of each chapter is a set of reflection/discussion questions. You could certainly work through these questions all by yourself. But it will be more meaningful and fun to read the book and discuss the questions with a friend. I believe it will produce some rich conversations.

3. *Complete the two assignments.* Embedded in the book are two life-shaping assignments. The first is to complete a Life Purpose Statement. That can sound daunting, but I will walk you through the steps to craft your statement. Second, at the end of the book, I will encourage you to write a Life Manifesto. This is a set of core values that will guide how you "do" life.

However you approach the book, it's my prayer that the chapters that follow will enrich your one life.

Introduction

YOUR. ONE. LIFE. When you string those three words together and slow down long enough to truly ponder them, they are quite sobering. In the entire history of humanity, no one has had or ever will have a life exactly like yours. And you get only one shot at your one and only life. Unlike your DVR, your life doesn't come with a Rewind button. There is no reincarnation, no do-over, no mulligan, and no second go-round.

Life is filled with moments and episodes that you will never live through again.

- ► Your senior year in high school
- ► Your wedding day
- ► Your thirteenth anniversary
- ► Your vacation last year
- ► Your lunch with a friend last week
- ► Your thirties
- ► Your child's first day of school
- ► Your forty-sixth birthday
- ► YESTERDAY

No matter what your age, you've already passed many life moments. You've lived through days, events, decisions, vacations, problems, special occasions, years, and seasons that you will never get back. They're done! You might carry the memory of them, but you can't turn back time and relive them. They are done . . . complete . . . past . . . over . . . closed . . . finito. And yet, time just keeps marching on.

Actually, when you think about it, life is a string of moments. But make no mistake, there is coming a moment that is the mother of all moments. You will take a final breath, your heart will beat for the last time, and *your one life* will be over. Yes, your life has an expiration date.

In that moment, you won't be done as a person, because you have a soul that will continue to live on past your earthly death. But your moment of death will close the book on the one and only life you'll ever have on this planet.

You see, the truth is, we're all "terminal." Emery, my eight-year-old granddaughter, recently reminded me of this sobering reality. We do cousin camp with our granddaughters each year, and I kiddingly asked them, "Do you guys think we will still be doing cousin camp when you're thirty?" Without any hesitation, Emery fired back, "Yes, if you and Nana aren't dead." In case you're wondering, she gets her brutally honest personality from her nana.

It's easy for us to think and act and live as though we're going to be here forever. But let me gently remind you, the death rate in your town or city is 100 percent. How is that for a warm, fuzzy thought to begin a book? None of us is exempt, and none of us will escape. In Ecclesiastes 8:8, Solomon gives us a sober reminder: "None of us can hold back our spirit from departing. None of us has the power to prevent the day of our death."

So the question is not "if" but "when." The Bible says that the Lord has numbered our days, but He has never revealed His spreadsheet. I don't know the number of my days, and you don't know the number of your days. Your departure flight from this life will not be delayed. Your one and only life on this planet had a beginning, and it will have an ending. Your death certificate is as certain as your birth certificate.

There's a lot we don't know about the number of our days. When will my number be up? Where will it happen? How will it happen? But this much I know for sure: your number is one less today than it was yesterday.

You didn't ask to be born, and you can't get out of dying. What you do in between, you have a lot of say over. What you do in between is called your *life*.

Life . . . let that word sink in for a moment. What an incredible gift. If you're a Christ follower, you believe and know that your life is not a random accident or cosmic coincidence. The Bible clearly declares God as the author of life. I love Eugene Peterson's paraphrase of Psalm 139:15.

> You know exactly how I was made, bit by bit,
> how I was sculpted from nothing into something. (MSG)

Think about that. God sculpted you from nothing into something. And He breathed life into your body and stamped you with the *imago Dei*. God custom-designed a life just for you. It is *your* life. He planned for you to be born at a certain time in history. He intricately designed your body and personality and intelligence and gifts with divine purpose. He gave you relationships and an ethnic culture so that you could belong.

But you aren't passive when it comes to your life. You are responsible for your life; you're the steward of your life. You will someday give an account to God for your one and only life. You have limitless options for what you could do with your life—what you think about, what you spend your time doing, what you spend your money on, what you choose to love, what matters to you, and what decisions you make. It's easy for us to get distracted and swept along in the current of everyday life. We can click through our days without really taking the time to ask where we're going and how we're living.

You have been given this incredible gift called *life*. You have amazing options and opportunities, but the truth is, sometimes that can be stressful and confusing. How are you supposed to live?

How do you make good choices? How do you not squander this gift? How do you not suck at life?

Maybe you're starting to get stressed out right now as you read those questions. Can I encourage you to relax and take a deep breath? I've got great news for you.

The Bible says that everything you need for life and godliness, you already have (2 Pet. 1:3).

The Bible is not a book that just tells us how to know God and love God. It's also a book about life. And God says to you and to me, "I have provided everything you need to live a rich and amazing life."

Before you turn the page, I want you to put down this book and head out to your garage. Next, I want you to grab a shovel. Now, get in your car and drive to your local cemetery. You'll need about six hours and exactly 1,405 shovelfuls of dirt . . . to dig a grave. By the way, don't forget to get permission from those in charge at the cemetery.

What I just described to you is what Michael Yankoski did one day. He literally dug a grave by hand and then lay down in the grave. With the cold dirt against the back of his head, Michael crossed his arms across his chest and closed his eyes.

When asked by the cemetery workers why he would do such a crazy thing, Michael said, "It's hard to explain. I'm trying to come to grips with my own mortality, I guess."[1]

Maybe you don't need to literally dig a grave, but every single one of us needs to come to grips with our mortality . . . with our one and only life on this planet.

Staring our own mortality in the face is good for us. But it isn't enough. We must also learn how to master the art of living. So, let's get started.

Part 1

CRAFTING
the LIFE
YOU LONG
to LIVE

It's Later Than
It's Ever Been

It is not the length of life, but the depth.

RALPH WALDO EMERSON

CAN YOU HEAR IT? You might have to turn off your TV. You will definitely have to put down your smartphone. If you get still and quiet, you can hear it right now. The sound is faint, but it is real. Because of the speed and noise of life, we rarely hear it or acknowledge it. The truth is, we don't like to hear it. We don't want to hear it. When we stop long enough to hear it, it makes us uncomfortable and forces us to ponder things we would rather not think about.

What I'm talking about is the ticking clock of your life. In quiet moments, you can hear the subtle sweep of the second hand relentlessly counting down the minutes of your life.

Psalm 90:12 says it like this:

> Teach us to realize the brevity of life,
> so that we may grow in wisdom.

Another translation of that verse says, "Teach us to number our days, that we may gain a heart of wisdom" (NIV).

One translation of that verse is a sober reminder about the brevity of life, and the other is a challenge to be intentional about our days. Both are important for living well.

Psalm 90 became especially real to me on a cold March night in Vail, Colorado. Some friends of ours were out of town but were gracious enough to let my wife, Connie, and me stay in their beautiful home while I worked with a church in the area. About 10:30 p.m., I crawled into bed. Normally, I can fall asleep within minutes. But that night something was different. I'm not quite sure how to explain it, but I just wasn't feeling like myself. After a few minutes of tossing and turning in bed, I decided to get up and see if moving around would help me feel better. Once I was out of bed, I knew something was wrong. I felt like I couldn't keep my balance, my hands were tingling, and my heart was racing and felt like it was about to burst out of my chest. Also, I felt like I couldn't think straight. My thoughts felt disconnected. I turned to my wife, who was already in bed, and said, "I think you should probably call an ambulance." Apparently my words were a bit slurred. I vaguely remember stumbling down the stairs and sitting on an ottoman in the living room.

Within just a few minutes, the EMTs arrived. In those minutes that they were working on me, I knew something was wrong but had no idea how serious it was. And even though there were people and medical equipment swirling all around me, I began to have very lucid thoughts about my life and the uncertainty of whether I would live to see another day. Also, in those moments, God provided a supernatural peace that dissipated any anxiety and fear. It was surreal. If it was God's plan that the second hand of my life stopped ticking that night, I was at peace and ready.

Connie had called a good friend who pastored a church in the area. He rushed right over and was with us as the ambulance took me to the Vail hospital.

I remember lying on the gurney in a holding area at the hospital. My pastor friend said, "Well, the good news is that they brought you here to the Vail hospital. If it was serious, they would take you to Denver." Within five seconds of him uttering those words, a nurse walked up and said, "We aren't really equipped to deal with neurological issues, so we're sending you to Denver." I remember looking up at my pastor friend and saying, "Your pastoral care skills suck."

So, they loaded me back into an ambulance, and we followed a snowplow down the mountain to Denver. As you've probably figured out, I survived and it ended up not being a heart attack or a life-altering stroke. It was determined that I had suffered a TIA, commonly referred to as a ministroke. There was no permanent brain damage (although some people might disagree), and within a couple days I was out of the hospital.

All Time Is Not Created Equal

When you live through episodes like the one I just described, the sweep of the second hand isn't faint and subtle. It screams at you and grabs you by the throat.

It reminds me of another verse in the Bible about time. In some of the modern translations, Ephesians 5:16 says to "make the most of every opportunity." But I memorized this verse many years ago in the King James Version, which translates the verse this way: "Redeeming the time, because the days are evil."

The idea behind the word *redeem* is to "purchase" or "buy up." When I make a purchase, it's a deliberate, intentional transaction. I'm exchanging some of my money for a product. In the same way, when it comes to my life, I'm regularly exchanging my time for something. The question is, Am I exchanging my time for that which is most valuable?

Interestingly, the Greeks had two different words for time: *chronos* and *kairos*. We get our word *chronological* from *chronos*. This is how we normally think of time. It's the actual seconds and minutes. It's a quantitative word. But that is not the word used in Ephesians 5:16. Paul very deliberately uses the root word *kairos*. *Kairos* is more qualitative and speaks more to the "right" moment or opportunity. Let me explain it like this. Every hour is the same when it comes to *chronos*. It's an exact measurement of sixty minutes, or 3,600 seconds. But not every hour is the same when it comes to *kairos*. Not every hour (*chronos*) provides equal opportunity (*kairos*) for using our time well.

Paul is challenging us to be intentional to buy up as many *kairos* opportunities as possible. Why? Because we have only one shot at this life, and because, as Paul says, "the days are evil." Living in the twenty-first century, we have unlimited options for how we spend our time.

When I think about moving from simply marking time (*chronos*) to maximizing time (*kairos*), the word that comes to mind is *clarity*. Clarity comes from understanding God's purposes and also through the process of self-discovery. God's eternal purposes and truth are universal and apply to all of us. But within the guardrails of God's timeless purposes, I need to discern my unique gifts, passions, values, and calling. That kind of clarity will point me toward a *kairos* kind of life.

None of us ever sets out to squander our life. No one ever plans to live a regret-filled life. As we begin this journey, I want to challenge you to put a stake in the ground declaring that you are going to tenaciously chase after a *kairos* kind of life. None of us will do it perfectly, and we're going to need to extend ourselves some grace along the way.

Maybe the most dangerous word in the English language is *someday*. Many of us suffer from the "someday syndrome." Someday I'll make things right with my mom. Someday I'll take that trip. Someday I'll have more time for the kids. Someday I'll get in shape. Someday I'll slow down. Someday I'll talk to my friend about Jesus. Someday I'll go back to school. In fact, why don't you fill in the blank. Someday, I'll _____.

What "someday" represents is a longing for more *kairos* moments. But the problem with "someday" is that it can rob us of "this day."

Obstacles to a Great Life

This book is my attempt to try to share how to live a *kairos* life of great purpose and deep satisfaction. As I honestly observe my own life and the lives of others, I believe there are two primary obstacles that get in the way. The first obstacle is what I would call passivity or drift. We just get caught in the current of culture and everyday life and are swept along without really asking, "Is this the way I want to live?" We don't take the time to really evaluate what we believe and then chart a clear course for the kind of life we deeply long to live. And I am unapologetically asking you to step back and take a more macro look at your life. Where is it headed? What trajectory are you on? What are your values? If you play the movie of your life forward, what kind of final scene does it have? I hope these chapters can help you take greater ownership of and responsibility for the only life you get.

The second obstacle has to do with the issue of courage. When I look in the rearview mirror at more than sixty years of life, one of my deepest regrets has to do with the issue of courage. That sentence was way harder for me to write than I thought it would be. In fact, it took a little while to muster the courage to admit my lack of courage.

They don't give medals for chickening out, backing down, getting cold feet, not taking a stand, backpedaling, or wimping out. The honest truth is, I am not a naturally courageous person. When I think of the word *courage*, there are a couple other words that aren't lagging far behind: *risk* and *pain*. And generally speaking, I am not a fan of either. I seek to mitigate risk and minimize pain. Regretfully, there have been many moments when I have let fear triumph over courage.

When I examine the Bible, I see that the life of absolute devotion to Christ always involves some demonstration of courage. Just mark it down. Somewhere along your journey Jesus will call you to take the risk of being courageous. Living for God's purposes will most certainly put you at odds with the world system. And staying true to your unique purpose will put you in the place of disappointing people you care about. There are many voices in your life that are more than happy to tell you how you should live and what you should give your time and energy to. But it's not their life . . . it is *your* life. And it takes courage to steward well your one life.

We usually think of courage in heroic, death-defying terms. But courage is usually much less dramatic. In fact, I'm convinced that several times a week your path and my path intersect opportunities to display courage, to actually act upon our values and priorities. Some courageous acts aren't public; they're just between us and God.

Before we go any further, I wanted to get the C word (courage) out on the table. To craft the life you want, you must get clarity about God's ultimate purposes in the world and also your unique purpose in this life. But clarity alone is not enough. Let that sink in. Acquiring more knowledge is not enough to achieve the life you deeply long for. Most of us are educated way beyond the level of our courage. It's going to take clarity *and* courage to stay the course and be true to yourself and God's purposes.

> Courage is what fills the gap between clarity and action.
> Courage is what fills the gap between knowing and doing.

Courage is not an issue of wiring but of willingness. It's not an issue of DNA but of heart. I have always found comfort and hope in a definition of courage frequently attributed to Ambrose Redmoon: "Courage is not the absence of fear, but rather the judgment that something else is more important than fear."[1]

My hope is that this week you will live with a greater awareness that the clock is ticking. And as you hear the faint sweep of the second hand, you'll be reminded that you get only one shot at this life. I don't know how many days are left in your account, but I do know that it's later than it's ever been.

REFLECTION/DISCUSSION QUESTIONS

1. On a scale of 1–10 (with 1 being low and 10 being high), how would you rate your current level of satisfaction with your life? Why did you give yourself that number?

2. Complete the following statement. Someday I hope to . . .

3. Take a few moments to do an honest reality check right now. Answer honestly the following three questions about your life:

   What's healthy?

   What's broken or stuck?

What's confused?

4. If your life ended this month, what would you regret?

2

Wherever You Go, There You Are

Most people don't lead their own
lives—they accept their lives.

JOHN KOTTER

WHEREVER YOU GO, there you are. That old saying is a poignant reminder that the one person you can never escape is yourself. The one person you can never run away from is *you*. You can't ever move to another city and leave yourself behind. Wouldn't it be nice if you were like a car? When you stop running smoothly or start breaking down or get old and beat up, you just take "you" down to the local dealer and trade "you" in for a new and improved model. No: wherever you go, there you are. You're stuck with yourself for the rest of your life. So you might as well get comfortable hanging out with "you."

Let's say you sleep seven hours per day. That means you have 119 hours every single week that you spend awake with yourself. The amount of time you'll spend with your spouse or your best friend or your co-worker doesn't even come close.

With those 119 hours, you are responsible and accountable for leading yourself. In the words of Henry Cloud, we are ridiculously in charge of our lives (see title of Cloud's book *Boundaries for Leaders: Results, Relationships, and Being Ridiculously in Charge*). Others can support, care for, encourage, instruct, challenge, rebuke, and mentor me, but I must lead myself. If you're a Christ follower, the Bible says that on the other side of this life you will stand before God at the judgment seat of Christ. This experience is not a judgment of sin. The penalty for our sins was paid by Jesus on the cross. The judgment seat of Christ is a judgment of rewards. There's a lot we don't know about the specifics of this judgment, but one thing we know with absolute certainty is that I will give an account for my life and you will give an account for yours. No one can stand in for me or take my place.

These realities raise the stakes of self-leadership. Several times a day, every day, you and I have self-leadership opportunities. God hardwired you with a "decider." And you use your decider multiple times every single day. You get to decide how you'll spend your money, whom you'll be in relationship with, how you'll spend your time, what you will think about, and whom you'll worship. Sometimes these self-leadership moments are small and mundane. At other times, they're big and dramatic and life-altering.

Lucid Clarity

This reality reminds me of a young man in the Bible who had a defining self-leadership moment. We meet him in the well-known story of the prodigal son. The point of the story is to shine the spotlight on God's grace toward us in our brokenness and rebellion. When the prodigal son returns home and his father runs to meet him, it's the only time in the Bible that God is ever pictured running.

But prior to this emotional and grace-filled reunion between a loving father and a rebellious son, there's a self-leadership moment that changes everything.

This younger son, impatient and impetuous, doesn't want to wait for his dad to die to get ahold of his inheritance. So in a moment of brash disrespect, he comes to his dad and says, "I want my share of the estate now." Even more surprising is that the dad goes for it.

The Bible then says that this son packs his bags and heads off for the distant country. His pockets are full and his dreams are big. He has life by the tail. He's free from all the restrictions and rules of home. He can do what he wants when he wants, and he's got the cash to pay for it.

But then come those tragic words: he "squandered his wealth in wild living" (Luke 15:13 NIV). We don't know the sequence of events, and we don't know how long it takes, but we do know he squanders every dime. The party lifestyle comes to a screeching halt.

Then, to make matters worse, a famine hits. So he's in a desperate situation, in part because of his own foolishness and in part because of a circumstance he had no control over.

I can imagine some of the thoughts that might have crossed his mind. "There's no way I'm going home. Face my dad? Forget it. I'll just get a job and climb out of this hole I've dug for myself." But the only job he can get is feeding pigs. That is disgusting in many cultures, but to a Jew, it was even more deplorable. Pigs were considered unclean and defiled, not just literally but also religiously. No self-respecting Jew would ever take such a job. It gets even worse; he takes the job and the famine is so bad that the Bible says "he longed to fill his stomach with the pods that the pigs were eating" (Luke 15:16 NIV). Even the pig slop starts looking pretty tasty.

And then comes the defining moment of self-leadership. I like the way the King James Version reads, because everything begins to change with the words "and when he came to himself" (v. 17). He has a moment of lucid clarity. He knows that back home even his dad's employees have more than enough to eat. In that moment, he decides to return home. He uses his God-given "decider" to change the trajectory of his life. He doesn't have to stay on the path he's on. His mistakes of the past don't have to define his future.

Another very insightful moment happens as he plans his return home. He rehearses what he will say to his dad. "Father, I have sinned against both heaven and you, and I am no longer worthy of being called your son. Please take me on as a hired servant" (vv. 18–19).

I love how this son takes full responsibility for his actions. I love the fact that he doesn't blame his upbringing or his friends or even the famine. Blame deflects personal responsibility and hinders us from good self-leadership. In their book *It's Not My Fault*, Henry Cloud and John Townsend say, "Blame is a sort of comfort food for the soul. It diverts us from the effort of owning responsibility."[1]

In every life there come moments when we, like the prodigal son, must come to ourselves and realize self-leadership is a choice. I must take responsibility for my one and only life. I must put down my "victim card" and own my feelings, my reactions, my attitudes, my motives, and my direction.

It's All about Self-Leadership

John Kotter said, "Most people don't lead their own lives—they accept their lives."[2] I think what Kotter is saying is that rather than exerting good self-leadership, most people take a more passive approach. They get caught up in the current of everyday life and passively get swept along to an unwanted destination. As another author put it, "We have forgotten that the natural foe to life is not a distant death, but a present, in-the-moment detachment from living."[3]

Perhaps the greatest verses in all the Bible about self-leadership are found in Deuteronomy 30. In the first ten verses, God extends an invitation to an abundant, blessed life. He says that if the Israelites will return to Him, He will restore their fortunes, increase their number, protect them from their enemies, prosper them, and give them bumper crops.

Right on the heels of this amazing offer, God speaks to self-leadership:

Now what I am commanding you today is not too difficult for you or beyond your reach. It is not up in heaven, so that you have to ask, "Who will ascend into heaven to get it and proclaim it to us so we may obey it?" Nor is it beyond the sea, so that you have to ask, "Who will cross the sea to get it and proclaim it to us so we may obey it?" No, the word is very near you; it is in your mouth and in your heart so you may obey it. (Deut. 30:11–14 NIV)

This abundant, rich, satisfying, fulfilling, meaningful, joy-filled life is accessible and available. In the words of Deuteronomy 30, it's not too difficult, and it's not out of reach. It is close at hand and available.

Second Peter 1:3 says, "By his divine power, God has given us everything we need for living a godly life." Everything! The life God has for me is not dependent on my income, my job description, my neighborhood, my looks, or my portfolio. I have every resource I need to live a rich and purposeful and satisfying life. So as we are just beginning this journey together, I encourage you to take a deep breath, relax, and slow down.

You can't do this in a hurry. You can't do this while you're sitting at a red light. You need some time to sit with yourself and with God. You need to honestly ask yourself, "What is the trajectory of my life? Am I truly giving my life to the things that I say are most important to me? What must change in order to live the life God has for me?"

Whenever you use Google Maps, you first punch in the desired destination. And then Google Maps builds a route for the best way to get there. But the key is knowing where you are now. You can't get where you want to go if you don't know where you are.

It's easy for us to live in self-deceit. I can always justify the way I'm living.

The French author François Fénelon said, "We have an amazing ability to self-deceive. Your self-interest hides in a million clever disguises."[4]

That's why it might be helpful to have an unhurried conversation with your spouse or a good friend. Get some honest feedback about what they observe in your life.

Start Changing the Story You're Telling Yourself

We all talk to ourselves. All day long we're telling ourselves stories about why someone didn't speak to us or what was behind their text message. All day long we're telling ourselves stories about why we got the promotion or why we need a new car. You are in constant conversation with yourself.

In Psalm 43:5, the psalmist talks to himself. In a moment of self-leadership, he redirects his soul.

> Why, my soul, are you downcast?
>   Why so disturbed within me?
> Put your hope in God,
>   for I will yet praise him,
>   my Savior and my God. (NIV)

In 1 Samuel 30:6, when David finds himself in a very difficult moment, the Bible says, "David strengthened himself in the Lord his God" (ESV). That is good self-leadership. The story I want to encourage you to start telling yourself is that you are ridiculously in charge of your life. God has given you everything you need to live an amazing, abundant life. It's not enough to change the story you're telling yourself; you must begin to take steps of good self-leadership. You must turn your face toward life and lean in to it. As we've already talked about, we get only one shot at our lives on this planet. Every day spent is one we will never get back.

When I think of *leaning in*, I think of the 100-meter Olympic race. As runners approach the finish line, they strain and literally lean in to the finish line with every fiber of their being. That is how I want to live my life. And it starts with self-leadership.

That might mean that we have to stop blaming others, stop playing the victim, and stop making excuses for why we can't live the life we want. As Benjamin Franklin said, "He that is good at excuses is seldom good at anything else."[5]

So don't let yourself off the hook. Don't give yourself a free pass. Don't rationalize or make excuses. Take responsibility. Start leading yourself.

Remember, today's decisions determine tomorrow's destiny.

One final word: it's never too late to start. No matter how dark your past or how much life you've squandered, you can start today. Right now! Our God is the God of the fresh start. So, put a stake in the ground and use your God-given "decider." Commit that from this day forward you are going to take extreme responsibility and practice good self-leadership.

REFLECTION/DISCUSSION QUESTIONS

1. When was a moment in your life that you "came to yourself" and made a life-altering change?

2. Answer the following two questions as a way to honestly take stock of your life:

   What's missing?

   What must change?

3. How would you describe your self-talk? What story are you constantly telling yourself?

4. Where do you tend to give yourself a free pass? In other words, where do you tend to come up with excuses or rationalize?

3

Plan, but Don't Presume

Distinguish between problems to
solve and tensions to manage.

ANDY STANLEY

IT WAS A BEAUTIFUL SUMMER DAY in Colorado. I was making the two-hour drive up the mountain to Vail. All of a sudden, I saw one of those huge electronic signs letting me know that a portion of I-70 was closed for a construction project and would require a detour.

Colorado, it seems, has only two seasons: winter and construction.

So hitting a construction zone or detour is almost a daily experience. It's mildly annoying. However, when the sign said the detour was an hour and fifteen minutes, I shot right past mildly annoyed and went straight to "you've gotta be kidding me." This was not in my plan for the day. No one checked with me to see if I would mind a detour. Nowhere in my calendar did I set aside time for an hour-long delay. As I got closer to the detour, there were probably sixty semis parked in single file on the shoulder of the highway. I have a feeling that some of those drivers may have said something more colorful than "you've gotta be kidding me."

As I exited I-70, it's possible that I had a few unkind thoughts running through my head about the highway department. The detour put me onto a two-lane road I had never traveled before. Within five minutes of starting my detour, I found myself in some spectacular mountain scenery. But I was too preoccupied with the implications of my delayed arrival to really take notice.

It was also irritating that the RVs and camping trailers couldn't go normal speeds over the winding and steep road. Sometimes we were slowed to a snail's pace, traveling no more than 10 or 15 mph. About fifteen minutes into the detour, I remember making the conscious decision to just relax, look around, and enjoy the beauty and adventure of a road I had never traveled. The longer I drove, the more spectacular and pristine the scenery became. I drove through Fremont Pass, which is 11,318 feet in elevation. It was just above the tree line and provided a breathtaking panoramic view of the valleys and mountain peaks.

That detour became the highlight of my day. What started off as a major inconvenience ultimately became a gift. My unwanted detour turned to unexpected delight.

God Is a Planner

I don't know about you, but I have a long history of resisting and resenting detours. By personality, I am a bit of a planner. On more than one occasion, my kids have accused me of being OCD. I think it sounds nicer to say I like to prepare.

By the way, I think God is a bit of a planner. He's guiding history toward His predetermined conclusion. History is not a random collection of events to which God reacts. The Bible is the written record of God creating and executing His plan.

And that same Bible encourages us to plan. There is nothing particularly noble or spiritual about flying by the seat of our pants.

When talking about the cost of being a disciple, Jesus said,

But don't begin until you count the cost. For who would begin construction of a building without first calculating the cost to see if there is enough money to finish it? (Luke 14:28)

Only a fool would rush into a building project without a set of blueprints, a cost analysis, and a construction game plan. We've all paid the price of impulsively rushing into something without taking the time to create a plan.

In Proverbs 24:27, Solomon says,

> Do your planning and prepare your fields
> before building your house.

I had a plan for my trip to Vail that day. I had a plan for when I would leave and when I would arrive. I had a plan for making a couple calls on my way up the mountain. I planned to have enough gas for the trip. Planning is good. Planning is wise. Planning is essential. In fact, the Bible links planning to success and prosperity:

> Good planning and hard work lead to prosperity,
> but hasty shortcuts lead to poverty. (Prov. 21:5)

Planning vs. Presumption

So the Bible absolutely affirms the value of a good plan, until that plan becomes presumption. *Presumption* is defined as the "audacious (even arrogant) behavior that you have no right to."[1]

God put a limit on our planning. Whenever our planning presumes upon the future, we've gone beyond the limits of appropriate planning. The boundary line of planning is the presumption of thinking and believing we can control the future. We can create our plans and hold them so tightly that we forget to allow for the myriad of things we don't control that can interrupt our plans.

James gives us a very appropriate warning about presumption in our planning:

> Look here, you who say, "Today or tomorrow we are going to a certain town and will stay there a year. We will do business there and make a profit." How do you know what your life will be like tomorrow? Your life is like the morning fog—it's here a little while, then it's gone. What you ought to say is, "If the Lord wants us to, we will live and do this or that." Otherwise you are boasting about your own pretentious plans, and all such boasting is evil. (James 4:13–16)

Luke 12 provides us with a case study of a man who crossed over the line from appropriate planning to inappropriate presumption. When things are going well and there's money in the bank and gas in the car and you're current with your bills and your portfolio is growing at a double-digit pace annually, you can easily be lulled into a false sense of being in full control.

In the parable in Luke 12, Jesus tells the story of a successful businessman who's making money hand over fist. He has to keep expanding and building bigger warehouses (barns). At the pinnacle of his success, one day he leans back in his office chair and says to himself, "My friend, you have enough stored away for years to come. Now take it easy! Eat, drink, and be merry!" (v. 19).

In the very next verse, we hear heaven's response to this man's arrogance and presumption. God says, "You fool! You will die this very night. Then who will get everything you worked for?" (v. 20).

Wow. The world would call this guy a business mogul, and I'm sure he would have been on the cover of *CEO Magazine*. Notice in the story that God doesn't call him wicked or dishonest or evil. Yet God does call him a fool. Nowhere in the story do we read that this man had mistreated his employees or scammed customers or cut ethical corners. He is certainly driven, ambitious, entrepreneurial, and shrewd. Yet God calls him a fool. For all his business savvy and entrepreneurial genius, he makes a supreme miscalculation.

He lives as though this life is all there is, and he acts as though he's in control of the future.

His strategic plan is to launch the business, work the business, grow the business, expand the business, sell the business, and retire on easy street. He's building a great big nest egg and an inflation-proof retirement portfolio. By most everyone's standards, this guy is living the dream. But God has a different assessment.

This story poignantly demonstrates the illusion of control. The rich CEO is used to being in charge and controlling everything in his world. The issue here is not his success or wealth, it is largely about presumption and misplaced priorities.

His self-talk drips with smugness and self-congratulation: "I've got all the bases covered. I've planned for all the possible contingencies. I am set for life." There's a country song that was wildly popular several years ago. It was called "Live Like You Were Dying" and is the story of a guy in the prime of his life who sits down with the doctor and gets the bad news about his health. His world is rocked as he realizes that he isn't in control. All his plans get changed in a moment. All it takes is to see that little spot on the X-ray or to get a pink slip or to have a drunk driver pull over into your lane.

As I write this book, we are in the throes of a global pandemic. In February 2020, most of us were rocking along like the businessman in Luke 12. We had it good and we were living the "eat, drink, and be merry" lifestyle. We had the illusion of control, and it seemed as if all the indicators were for a life that was up and to the right. Then we entered March 2020, and *everything* changed.

When you stop and think about it, there's so little in this life that we really control.

The older I get, the more acutely aware I am that life is fragile and control is only a mirage. None of us has the guarantee of another year or even another day.

As I conclude this chapter, I want to give you two challenges that will serve you well as you go through this book: take time to plan and hold your plans loosely.

Create a Plan

As you work through this book, you're going to be challenged to take some time to plan. Planning is nothing more than thinking about your future and developing a desirable road map.

Right now, I know what some of you are thinking. In fact, I can hear Connie's voice in my head (that happens a lot). "Not all of us have our life mapped out three years in advance. Some of us are more spontaneous and impulsive and free-spirited." Years ago, before we did everything on our smartphones, in an attempt to help my wife organize and plan her life better, I bought her a quite expensive Day-Timer. What can I say? I'm just a romantic and a giver. I'm not sure she ever used it, and within a couple weeks it was lost, never to be found again. (That's code for "I'm pretty sure she threw it in the trash.")

So I understand that some of us are not planners by nature. But before you give yourself a free pass to blow off the planning challenge, I want to remind you of the words of Proverbs 14:8:

> The wisdom of the prudent is to give thought to their
>   ways,
>   but the folly of fools is deception. (NIV)

Wise people think about their ways. Wise people plot the trajectory of their lives. Wise people are clear about where they're headed and create a plan to get there.

Hold Your Plans Loosely

So when you come across those places in the book where you are challenged to do a bit of planning, let me encourage you to take that seriously.

Planning is helpful; presumption is harmful. When you're a follower of Christ, you have to stay aware that God holds the trump card to your life. He has "veto power" over your plans.

> You can make many plans,
>   but the LORD's purpose will prevail. (Prov. 19:21)

The key word of this verse is *but*. That is the place of tension and uncertainty. God has a long history of interrupting people's plans. He is the divine disruptor. I believe He does so for some very clear reasons.

- ► He has a plan for my life and purposes for the world that I don't know about. To accomplish His purposes, at times He must blow up my plans.
- ► He wants me to learn to trust Him completely. Sometimes when I'm rocking along through life and everything is good, I can start trusting in myself and in my plan (think rich businessman in Luke 12). It's been my experience that my faith and trust grow when my world gets rocked.
- ► Because God is a loving and benevolent Father, He knows what is best. As loving parents, we've all experienced the need to step in and change the plans of our kids. God does the same in our lives, but He never does it for our harm—He does it for our good. When you trust that God is good and working for you, you don't have to resent the detours.

The trip to Vail that day taught me a valuable lesson. I knew where I wanted to go. I was clear about my goal, and I had a good plan for getting to my desired destination. Ultimately, even though I had a detour, I ended up where I planned to go. And I never would have experienced the rich beauty of that day if someone else hadn't disrupted my plans and given me the gift of a detour. Sometimes the richest adventures in life are the detours you didn't plan to take.

REFLECTION/DISCUSSION QUESTIONS

1. When was there a time that lack of planning got you into trouble or caused problems?

2. At the heart of presumption is the faulty belief that we are in control. How much do you struggle with "control issues"? Where does that show up in your life?

3. Where could you do better when it comes to planning? Does an area of life come to mind?

4. Identify a time when God detoured your life. What was the result?

The Most Important Word in the Bible

You didn't create yourself, so there is no way you
can tell yourself what you were created for.

RICK WARREN

IF YOU HAD TO SELECT ONE WORD in the Bible as the most important, what would it be? And you can't choose *God* or *Jesus*.

I suspect that if we did a survey of Christians, these would be some of the top vote-getter words:

salvation	forgiveness	resurrection
grace	heaven	worship
gospel	cross	truth

I suspect very few of us would choose the word that I believe should be the top candidate for the most important word in the Bible. It's a word that is tossed around a lot in Christian circles but rarely used by those who don't follow Jesus. It's found frequently in our worship songs, and it easily rolls off our tongues when we pray. Yet I suspect most of us would have a hard time defining it. I'm talking about a word that describes God's essence. It expresses the sum total of God's attributes. The word that might be most important in the Bible is *glory*.

In 1643, the English Parliament pulled together some of the greatest theologians and biblical scholars of the day. These men met at Westminster Abbey over a period of five years. One of the results of their meetings was a document called the Westminster Shorter Catechism. The catechism answered a series of doctrinal and theological questions. Question #1 was "What is the chief end of man?" Thousands of books have been written attempting to answer that all-important question. Surprisingly, the answer from these biblical scholars was just eleven words. "Man's chief end is to glorify God and enjoy Him forever."

This distinguished group of scholars and lifelong students of Scripture said the ultimate purpose for which man exists is to *glorify God*.

It's Not about You

As we begin to talk about crafting the life you long to live, the proper starting place isn't your preferences, it's God's purposes. The beginning point is not your dreams for your life but His destiny for your life. The discussion doesn't begin with your goals, it begins with God's glory.

We are part of something bigger than ourselves, bigger than our own personal dreams. We are not a random collection of individuals who just happened to show up on this planet at this time in history. You were created on purpose, and you have a calling that transcends chasing after the "good life." Life is way more than just your own personal pursuit of happiness and comfort.

If I handed you a tool that you had never seen before, the tool couldn't tell you its intended use. The designer and creator of that tool would have to reveal its purpose. According to Rick Warren, "You didn't create yourself, so there is no way you can tell yourself what you were created for."[1] The tool doesn't decide why it exists;

its creator defines its purpose. In the same way, your Creator has designed you with a purpose in mind.

To craft the life you want, you must discover why you were created. Only your Creator has the answer.

I want to break some news to you, and for some this is going to be a shock: *You are not the center of the universe.* I know that is a blow to your ego and maybe contrary to what your grandma told you. God doesn't exist for us; we exist for Him and to bring Him glory.

As Rick Warren writes in the opening line of *The Purpose Driven Life*, "It's not about you."[2] The central character of the Bible isn't me, and it isn't you. It is God Himself. History really is *His* story. It's God's story. It's the story of His love, His grace, His plan, His salvation, and ultimately, it is for His glory.

At the end of the day, life works so much better when I align myself with His story rather than try to fit Him in around the edges of *my* story. Even though God doesn't need me, the fact that He created me in His image and saved me and gives me a life of purpose in this world is mind-blowing. When you really get how big He is and how small you are, it doesn't minimize your significance, it makes it even greater. David beautifully articulates this perspective in Psalm 8:

> When I look at the night sky and see the work of your
> fingers—
> the moon and the stars you set in place—
> what are mere mortals that you should think about them,
> human beings that you should care for them? (vv. 3–4)

Moses Makes an Odd Request

So if my ultimate purpose is to glorify God, then I should probably understand what that means. And in order to understand how to glorify God, I must understand His glory.

In Exodus 33:18, Moses makes a very strange request. He says to God, "Now show me your glory" (NIV).

Of all the things he could have requested of God, why does he ask to see God's glory? What is glory? Glory is not easy to define or picture, like a table or a chair. It's more like trying to define beauty.

It might help us to understand a little about the Hebrew word used for glory in the Old Testament. It derives from a root word that has the basic meaning of "heavy" or "weighty."[3] The "weightiness" or abundance of God's amazing attributes make up His glory. Ancient Hebrews would refer to a rich person as "heavy in wealth," much as we might say someone is loaded. So when it comes to God, we could say He is heavy (or loaded) with power, splendor, beauty, and honor.

Here is my definition of the word *glory*. Glory is the manifestation of God's essence. It is the sum total of His majesty, sovereignty, holiness, love, power, and beauty put on display. When it's used as a verb ("to glorify"), it has the idea of bringing honor or worship or fame.

Let's go back to Exodus 33, where Moses asks God to show him His glory.

God says, "But . . . you cannot see my face, for no one may see me and live" (see v. 20). It's like God is saying, "Moses, you have no idea what you are asking."

Then God continues by basically saying this: "Moses, here's what I'm going to do. I'm going to place you in the crevice of a rock, and I'm going to cover you with My hand. And once I've passed by, I'm going to remove My hand and you will see the back side of My glory."

It's impossible to really wrap your mind around this bizarre scene.

The Bible says that Moses had a supernatural encounter with the presence and glory of God. When Moses came down off Mount Sinai, he wasn't aware that his face literally, physically radiated the glory of God. And the people were freaked out and didn't want to come near him. Moses's brief exposure to God's glory left him literally "shining."

Psalm 19:1 says, "The heavens declare the glory of God" (NIV). When you look into the night sky and see galaxies of planets and stars, it is God's glory put on display. When you feel the warmth of the sun's rays, it comes from a glowing ball of fire perfectly positioned ninety-three million miles away. David says that is God putting His glory on exhibit.

Jesus: Concentrated Glory

Now let's fast-forward to the New Testament. Do we see God's glory there? Yes, but it looks much different.

> The Word became flesh and made his dwelling among us. We have seen his glory, the glory of the one and only Son, who came from the Father, full of grace and truth. (John 1:14 NIV)

> The Son is the radiance of God's glory and the exact representation of his being, sustaining all things by his powerful word. (Heb. 1:3 NIV)

The picture that comes to my mind is that of a ray of light. A ray emanates from the sun itself; it has the same essence as the sun, but it's in a smaller dose. It's like buying concentrated laundry detergent. It has the full strength of regular detergent, but it's packed in a smaller size. In Jesus we see the glory of God in concentrated form.

Then, if you go to the very end of the Bible, you see the glory of God showing up again. In the next-to-last chapter in the Bible, Revelation 21, John is describing the New Jerusalem. It is an amazing heavenly city, and John says, "The city does not need the sun or the moon to shine on it, for the glory of God gives it light, and the Lamb is its lamp" (v. 23 NIV). The glory of God is the electrical power plant of heaven.

This theme of God's glory runs all the way through the Bible.

So What?

So how does God's glory play itself out in my life today?

In Colossians 1, the apostle Paul is talking about the fact that the gospel is not just for the Jews but for all people. He says,

> To them God has chosen to make known among the Gentiles the glorious riches of this mystery, which is Christ in you, the hope of glory. (Col. 1:27 NIV)

Paul describes something amazing that happens at the moment of conversion. Conversion is that moment when you make the choice, by faith, to receive Christ as your Lord and Savior. In that instant, the Bible says that the Holy Spirit comes to permanently indwell you.

Here is the difference between you and Moses. The glory of God temporarily got *on* him. At the moment of conversion, the glory of God permanently got *in* you.

How important is this? So important that Jesus said it would be better for the disciples that He go away. Think about that statement. What could be better than having Jesus hanging out *with* you? Having God's glory and presence in the person of the Holy Spirit *in* you.

Friends, that is a game changer. Let that soak in! If you are a Christ follower, you have this amazing gift of the presence of God as your constant companion.

Notice in Colossians 1:27 that Paul says Christ in you is the "hope of glory" (NIV). It's the appetizer, the down payment, the sampler platter of what we're going to experience in fullness in heaven.

So, how does God's glory impact me architecting my one life?

1. *It helps me understand "true north" in my life.* If I start each day with the question "How can I live my life in a way that brings God glory?" that leads me down a totally different path than asking myself, "How can I pursue my own dreams and happiness?" Perhaps the following questions would be good for us to ponder.
   - ▸ What does it look like to glorify God in the way I work?
   - ▸ What does it look like to glorify God in my marriage or in my friendships?
   - ▸ What does it look like to glorify God in how I spend my money?
   - ▸ What does it look like to glorify God with technology devices?

What if God's glory began to be a more conscious part of my day? What if I let His honor and glory become a driving force in every area of my life?

2. *As I seek to be more like Jesus, more and more of His glory is put on display.* Second Corinthians 3:18 says we "are being transformed into his image with ever-increasing glory, which comes from the Lord, who is the Spirit" (NIV).

This is the work of sanctification. The word translated as "transformed" here is actually *metamorphosis.* Slowly, day by day, I am transformed into His image with "*ever-increasing glory.*" From the inside out, the glory of God's being and character begins to have greater hold and power in my life.

People ought to see more glory in me this year than they saw last year. We are to be like the moon. It has no light or radiance of its own. It's simply the reflector of the sun.

3. *In everything I do, I am to point people toward God and make Him famous. I am to give Him honor and worship.* According to 1 Corinthians 10:31, God's glory is to be the driver of everything I do: "So whether you eat or drink or whatever you do, do it all for the glory of God" (NIV).

In the everyday, normal, common, mundane things of life, your calling is to *glorify* God. This is not some trite, banal platitude. This has real-life implications, and you need to settle this issue in your life once and for all. What is going to be the authority that determines the direction of your life? Is it going to be your own desires and pleasure? Is it going to be pop culture? Will your life navigation system be the values you grew up with? Or is it going to be God's purpose and glory? How you answer matters. Your answer sets the trajectory for your one and only life.

REFLECTION/DISCUSSION QUESTIONS

1. Take a few moments to reflect back on the story of how you came to Christ.

2. In your own words, describe what it means for you to live for God's glory. How does that impact choices you make and how you live?

3. Second Corinthians 3:18 says we "are being transformed into his image with ever-increasing glory, which comes from the Lord, who is the Spirit" (NIV). What are some ways that God is working in you and changing you?

4. If you really made the conscious decision to live for God's glory, how might that change some things in your life?

CHAPTER 5

Begin at the End

I intend to live forever. So far, so good.

EUGENE O'KELLY

IT'S EASY FOR US to live in denial about our mortality, but the psalmist gives us a good dose of reality in Psalm 90:10:

> Seventy years are given to us!
>   Some even live to eighty.
> But even the best years are filled with pain and trouble;
>   soon they disappear, and we fly away.

You probably won't find that verse in a Hallmark card.

I remember the first time I really encountered the stark reality of death. As a kid, I rarely ever thought about death. And I don't remember knowing anyone who had died, which might explain why I have no recollection of going to a funeral in my growing-up years.

However, when I was nineteen, I got asked not just to attend a funeral but to help with a funeral. I was a young aspiring pastor, and my wife and I were part of a team traveling through central California speaking at churches and doing youth events. This particular week our exotic travel itinerary had taken us to Kerman, California. The pastor of the church where I was speaking was actually the interim pastor and had been for the last fourteen years. Somehow, I don't think they were real serious about landing a permanent pastor.

That week an older gentleman in the church had passed away, so the pastor thought it would be good training for me to assist him with the funeral service. Little did I realize that his "good idea" was going to become one of the more traumatic experiences of my young ministry career.

It was an afternoon funeral, and the pastor asked me to read Scripture during the service. Easy enough. He also asked me to stand at the foot of the casket as people passed by at the end of the service. Easy enough.

The funeral got off to a bit of a rough start. You see, they had also asked my wife and her friend Diana to sing the opening song of the funeral. Easy enough. These young ladies were accomplished singers. So at 2:00 p.m., the start time for the funeral, they stood up and beautifully sang the song the family had requested. Just one problem. The family still had not arrived.

At about 2:10, once the family had arrived and taken their seats, Connie and Diana did an encore of their funeral song. The rest of the service went off without a hitch. Well, almost!

As planned, after the service was completed, those attending filed by the open casket to pay last respects to the deceased man. The second-to-last person to walk by the casket was this gentleman's sister. As she saw her brother lying in the casket, she was overcome with grief and blurted out, "You can't leave me." Then she reached down into the casket and put her arms around her brother and began to crawl into the casket. No, I am not kidding. She had one leg in the casket when the pastor and funeral director quickly came over and gently pulled her away. As they were walking away, the pastor turned his head away from this grieving sister and whispered to me, "Straighten up the body." No, I am not kidding. As I looked in the casket, I saw that she had managed to pull his body over to the side. He was almost lying on his side, his hair was messed up, and his glasses were sitting cockeyed on his face. I quickly nudged his body back into the middle of the casket and got the heck out of there, hoping the funeral director would comb his hair and straighten his glasses.

Staring Down Your Mortality

I hope you never have that kind of funeral experience, but it was good for me. And it's good for each of us to come face-to-face with our mortality. Did you know that "people are 40 percent more likely to help someone who is in need of help if they've just walked past a cemetery"?[1]

I wonder why that's the case? Maybe it's because the reminder of death recalibrates our perspective. Death has a way of shaking us out of our trancelike existence and reminding us that we won't always be here. Dr. Samuel Johnson (the author of the first English dictionary) once said, "Death wonderfully concentrates the mind."[2]

The truth of death should help us embrace the treasure of life. And the finality of death raises the stakes on your one and only life. As we have talked about, you get only one shot at this life and then, in the words of the psalmist, "we fly away."

Let's backtrack just a moment to the beginning of your life. When you were born, you were given a set of raw materials with which to craft an amazing life. You were given personality, energy, senses, dreams, DNA, skills, relationships, and imagination. Before the moment you "fly away," the life you build with those raw materials is largely up to you.

In a previous chapter, we talked about the fact that our lives are to be lived for the ultimate purpose of God's glory. Imagine for a moment that you're standing in front of a blank canvas. The edges represent God's glory. In other words, you want to paint a life within the boundaries of God's glory. The blank canvas represents limitless options and opportunities and experiences and unique expressions of a life that could bring glory to God. But let's be honest: a blank canvas can be intimidating.

For some of us, our life is a paint-by-numbers kit, and we paint the life somebody else has already mapped out for us. Others of us sort of float through life randomly throwing some colors on the canvas and hoping our life creates some kind of picture.

Defining Your Unique Life Purpose

The key to a unique masterpiece of a life is to discover our unique individual purpose within the broader purpose of God's glory. Once we have a clear picture of the life we were intended to live, we can go to work on actually painting (living) a rich, vibrant life.

The only way to adequately prepare for a great vacation is to first know the destination. Knowing the destination will help you know how much money to save, what clothes to pack, what flights to take, and what activities to plan for.

Once you're clear about your life purpose, it will help you know how to spend your time, allocate your resources, invest in relationships, plan your year, develop your skills, and best serve others. A life purpose also becomes a filter, helping you discern what you should say yes to and what you should say no to. You can do almost anything you want; you just can't do everything you want. Having a clear purpose and focused direction is like creating a budget for your one life. A budget establishes priorities and clarifies where your resources are going to be spent. If I know I have $168 coming in, I can decide in advance exactly how I will spend that money. In the same way, I also know that I will have 168 hours in the coming week. I can decide now how to invest those precious hours so I spend them doing things that matter.[3]

In his book *First Things First*, Stephen Covey talks about the clock and the compass. "The clock represents our commitments, appointments, schedules, goals, activities—what we do with, and how we manage, our time. The compass represents our vision, values, principles, mission, conscience, direction—what we feel is important and how we lead our lives."[4]

The compass is directional, the clock is managerial. The compass is about destination, the clock is about implementation. The compass is about the macro, the clock is about the micro. The compass is long term, the clock is short term.

A Clock and a Compass

The compass is about *kairos*, the clock is about *chronos*.

We talked about these two Greek words a little earlier. But remember, *kairos* is qualitative and is a compass word. *Kairos* drips with emotion, passion, purpose, value, and experience. When we ask someone if they had a good time on vacation, we're asking a *kairos* question.

For the purposes of this chapter, the most important thing to know about *kairos* and *chronos* is that *kairos* always comes first. *Chronos* (clock) is always to live in submission to *kairos* (compass).

I do a lot of coaching of leaders, and I see two common problems when it comes to the compass and the clock.

First, there are those who have never taken the time to clarify the ultimate picture they want to paint with their life. They've never crystallized and articulated for themselves what a successful, fruitful, abundant, God-honoring life would look like. When it comes to the target of their life, they've never identified the bull's-eye. And when there is no compass, the clock (your time) becomes a random collection of activities and experiences. In other words, people can't find their "way" in life when they don't know their "why" in life.

Second, there are people who are clear about what matters most to them, and they have articulated some kind of life purpose. But their challenge is that the clock (how they spend their time) isn't aligned with what they have declared is their purpose. These people need courage to align their clock so that it supports and facilitates their life purpose.

It all starts with defining true north (the compass) in your life.

At the end of this chapter, you're going to be given the challenge and opportunity to craft a Life Purpose Statement. Your personal purpose statement is your compass (true north). In a world that's spinning fast and changing rapidly, your true north is your fixed point of orientation.

Without a clear picture of the life we're called to live, our lives end up being marked by restless confusion, wasted energy, unnecessary pain, squandered opportunities, haunting regrets, and lack of fulfillment.

Let me leave you with this sobering example. Oscar Wilde was a man of incredible talent and potential. He was a poet, playwright, novelist, and critic. It brought him lots of money and notoriety. He experienced a level of success beyond his maturity to handle it. He would eventually die bankrupt and broken at age forty-six. Prior to his death, while sitting in prison, Wilde wrote these very sobering words of self-reflection:

> I must say to myself that I ruined myself, and that nobody great or small can be ruined except by his own hand. . . . Terrible as what the world did to me, what I did to myself was far more terrible still.[5]

Before you move on from this chapter, I want to challenge you to spend some time responding to the following questions. This exercise will replace the reflection/discussion questions for this chapter. Your answers to these questions will help inform the purpose statement you'll begin to draft at the end of the chapter. Let me encourage you to not only give these questions some serious reflection but also take the time to write out some of your thoughts.

- At the end of the day, what matters most to me?
- At my funeral, what three words or phrases do I want people to use when talking about me?
- What would I like my one-sentence epitaph to be?
- What changes would I make if I knew I had only one year left to live?

Life Purpose Statement

A Life Purpose Statement serves as the true north of your life. It's a way of declaring the direction of your life and why you were put on the earth. It's a clear expression of what you're giving your life to—the "must do" of your existence. As a Christ follower, your Life Purpose Statement must align with God's purposes, God's glory, and God's truth.

Don't get in a hurry when crafting your statement. It may take a few days or weeks to really clarify and refine. Here are a few pointers for crafting your own personal Life Purpose Statement:

- Spend some time in quiet reflection. Try to answer the following questions. At the end of the day, what really matters to me? What do I want my life to be about? At my funeral, what would I want people to say about me? As I think about the end of my life, what could cause me regret?

- Then do a brainstorming exercise. Come up with a list of words that you might want to include in your statement. Nouns could include *God, Jesus, people, family, leaders, life*, etc. Create a list of action words that you could consider using, like *impact, love, serve, lead, equip, challenge*, and *follow*. You might also want to include some adjectives or adverbs, like *courageously, focused, deeply, attentive, intentionally*, etc.

- Make sure these are words that you would use and that when somebody hears your Life Purpose Statement, they think the words you chose ring true of your personality and values.

- Now you can begin to create a draft statement. At this point, don't worry about length or wordsmithing. Also, remember (and this is really important) that this is not a vocational purpose statement. And it is not just for this season of life you are in currently. It is a *Life* Purpose

Statement. In creating a draft, I like to use language such as, "My purpose is . . ." or "I exist to . . ."

- Once you've created a draft statement, you can begin to refine and condense your statement into a clear and concise sentence. Every word matters. Remove any words that are redundant or unclear. This is not a marketing slogan to go on a website. This is for you! So choose clear over cute.

- Personally, I think the best Life Purpose Statements come in under twenty words. My Life Purpose Statement is just over twenty words, but it's easy for me to remember, so I've stuck with it. By way of example, I am sharing my Life Purpose Statement below.

- Some space is provided below for you to get started drafting your Life Purpose Statement.

Lance's Life Purpose Statement

To steward well my one life by
Loving God deeply,
Leading myself tenaciously,
Shepherding my family intentionally,
Coaching and serving leaders wisely.

Brainstorming Words Exercise

Noun/Object Words   Action/Descriptive Words

_____   _____

_____   _____

_____   _____

_____   _____

_____   _____

_____   _____

_____   _____

Life Purpose Statement Draft

_____

_____

_____

_____

_____

Life Purpose Statement

_____

_____

_____

_____

_____

_____

_____

_____

_____

_____

_____

_____

_____

_____

_____

_____

_____

_____

Part 2

LIFE'S OPERATING SYSTEM: A HEALTHY SOUL

CHAPTER 6

Are Souls Overrated?

You are not just a self; you are a soul.

DALLAS WILLARD

IF YOU NEVER SAW the little-known movie *Bedazzled*, you didn't miss much. But there is one intriguing scene where the devil, played by Elizabeth Hurley, offers Brendan Fraser seven wishes to use however he sees fit. The only stipulation is that he must give his soul to the devil, to which he responds, "I can't give you my soul." She asks, "What's the big deal? Have you ever seen your soul? Do you even know what it is?"

"Of course! It's that thing that . . . floats around." To which the devil replies, "Can I tell you something? Souls are overrated. They don't ever do anything. Has yours done anything for you so far? It's like your appendix. You won't even miss it."

Pausing for a moment, Fraser responds, "Hey, if it's so useless, how come you want it so much?"[1]

If you had followed me around and observed my life for many years, you would have concluded that I seemed to think souls are overrated. But in more recent years, I have come to believe with great conviction that paying attention to your soul (your inner life) is critical to living the life you long to live. You can't delegate or outsource the care of your soul. You and you alone are its keeper.

You Are the Keeper of Your Soul

Think of your soul like a seed. You didn't create the seed; it was gifted to you by God. Inside that seed is life and the potential of growth and fruit. But that seed has to be watered, nurtured, and cared for in order for the soul to flourish. That seed is also fragile and vulnerable to disease and attack. The seed of your soul must be protected and guarded. The point is that YOU are the gardener of the seed of your soul.

In 3 John 2, John writes, "Dear friend, I pray that you may enjoy good health and that all may go well with you, even as your soul is getting along well" (NIV). I'm intrigued by that last phrase, "even as your soul is getting along well." How would you know if your soul was getting along well? How would you know if your soul wasn't getting along well? If you were a lawyer and had to build a case for a healthy soul, what evidence would you present?

When John Wesley started "bands" (what we would call "small groups"), they had a very defined curriculum. They started their group meeting each week with the same question: "How is it with your soul?" I remember reading that question for the first time several years ago and thinking to myself, "I would have no idea how to answer that question."

For most of my life, "soul talk" was foreign to me. Theologically, I would have known that I had a soul and Jesus died for my soul. But it was not something that had much impact on my day-to-day living. Who had time to worry about their soul when there was so much to accomplish and achieve?

Pay Attention!

I have a long history of neglecting my soul, and it's only been in more recent years that I began to pay attention to my soul (inner life) and have been learning how to be the gardener of my soul.

But really, what is a soul and how do I care for it?

One day when Dallas Willard was talking about the value and mystery of our existence, he said, "You are not just a self; you are a soul. You're a soul made by God, made for God, and made to need God, which means you were not made to be self-sufficient."[2]

So it is not a stretch to say that your soul is the real you. You could be in an accident and have an arm amputated, but it doesn't change the essence of your soul. You could have a kidney transplant, but you are still YOU. Nothing has changed as far as your soul. Speaking from my own personal experience, you could even lose your hair and you still have the same soul. The essence of your soul is not defined by a body part. Sometimes in the Bible the word *soul* is synonymous with the person. Your soul far more defines who you are than your body does.

Maybe this overly simplistic illustration will help. Imagine that your body is your car. And now imagine that you represent your soul. You (your soul) sit behind the steering wheel. You determine how fast the car goes and when it stops. You determine when the oil is changed and the path the car takes.

The car (your body) is simply the vehicle that gets you from place to place.

Someday your body (your car) is going to wear out and die. But even when your heart beats for the last time and they pronounce you dead and stick your body in the ground, I've got good news. You are not really dead. Your soul (the real you) will be fully alive, and if you're a Christ follower, your death is simply the transition into heaven. As the apostle Paul said in 2 Corinthians 5:8, "We would rather be away from these earthly bodies, for then we will be at home with the Lord."

Think about how much effort and time we put into caring for our bodies. We primp, clean, groom, shampoo, wash, deodorize, manicure, comb, exercise, feed, paint, and perfume—all before 8:00 a.m. Yet no matter how hard we work to take care of our bodies, they are going to get old and weak and will die! Doesn't it make sense then that we would put as much energy into and focus on caring for our souls?

The idea of the soul is one of the most important concepts in the Bible, yet it's one of the hardest to define and explain. It's the "you" separate from your body. It's the immaterial, invisible part of you. It's your inner life. Your soul is the *unseen, eternal* self.

Let's unpack those two words, *unseen* and *eternal*.

Just because something is unseen doesn't mean it's unimportant. Your soul is much like the operating system running inside your computer and smartphone. It runs in the background and no one really sees it, but it is essential for making everything else work. The success and effectiveness of your software programs are 100-percent dependent on the operating system functioning properly. And all of the visible programs in your life are absolutely dependent on your soul functioning properly. Your operating system integrates all the different programs on your computer, and your soul integrates all the different components of your life and makes them work in a holistic manner.

When you have too many programs running, it can bog down your operating system. And when you have too much going on in your life, it can cause soul fatigue. A few years ago, I was coaching a leader who had been overloading his operating system (soul) so much and for so long that he hit the wall. And just like many do with their computer operating system, he ignored his soul until it crashed. As we started our coaching together, he said, "I'm not asking you to help me get back to where I was. I can't ever go back there again. I won't make it. I must recalibrate my life and establish a new normal." We worked together to help him push the Reset button on his life and soul.

Your soul is not only unseen but also eternal.

In Ecclesiastes 3, Solomon said that God has planted eternity in the human heart. It's one of the qualities that separates us from the rest of creation. Unlike with lions and tigers and bears (sorry, I just had a *Wizard of Oz* moment), God has uniquely wired into our DNA the ability to think about and ponder the future. We are the only creatures who have a belief that there is life after death. The soul can never fully be at home in this world because God planted a homing beacon in us called "eternity." And that homing beacon is a constant reminder that our soul's real home is not in this life but in an eternal existence with God.

Life Flows from the Inside to the Outside

There's a fundamental truth that runs like a thread all the way through the Bible. And that truth is that the flow of a healthy life is inside to outside.

Not only did Jesus model the inside-out life, but He also never wavered in His own teaching on this topic.

- ► "A tree is identified by its fruit. If a tree is good, its fruit will be good. If a tree is bad, its fruit will be bad" (Matt. 12:33).
  Principle: The root always dictates the fruit.
- ► "A good person produces good things from the treasury of a good heart, and an evil person produces evil things from the treasury of an evil heart" (Matt. 12:35).
  Principle: The invisible produces the visible.
- ► "For whatever is in your heart determines what you say" (Matt. 12:34).
  Principle: Your internal well determines your external words.
- ► "Yes, I am the vine; you are the branches. Those who remain in me, and I in them, will produce much fruit" (John 15:5).
  Principle: Life flows from the vine to the branches.

The harshest and most biting language Jesus uses in the New Testament had to do with this issue. Speaking to the religious leaders of His day, Jesus said, "For you are like whitewashed tombs—beautiful on the outside but filled on the inside with dead people's bones and all sorts of impurity. Outwardly you look like righteous people, but inwardly your hearts are filled with hypocrisy and lawlessness" (Matt. 23:27–28).

Focusing on our external life while our inner life languishes is like getting a facelift when we have a malignant tumor ravaging our body from within. We all know what it is to be the Pharisee and prop up an external image that doesn't match the reality of our soul.

In Proverbs 4:23, Solomon challenges us with these words: "Above all else, guard your heart, for everything you do flows from it" (NIV). Solomon says that you and I are to make it our top priority to guard our inner life. Why? Because *everything* we do flows from it. It is a law that God hardwired into the universe. The NLT says that you are to guard your heart "for it determines the course of your life."

A poorly managed interior life will lead to a poorly lived exterior life. An unhealthy root will always lead to unhealthy fruit. As Henry Cloud says, "We ignore our internal life, and as a result, we do not have the outside 'life' that we desire."[3]

So, how about it? Is your soul even on your radar? When is the last time you thought about your interior life? Is your soul buried under a life so full and hurried and noisy that you actually forgot it was there? You see, your soul will never fight for your attention.

That's why you and I have to learn the art of paying attention to our souls. In the following chapters, we'll explore your internal scripts, your family of origin, attitudes and assumptions, and also ways that you can keep your soul filled up and healthy. But it starts with awareness that you have a soul and learning to pay attention to it.

Whether concentrating while driving, listening to a professor in class, focusing on your pastor's sermon, being engaged when your kids are talking to you, or really being present with God when you pray, paying attention is one of life's hardest disciplines to learn. And learning to pay attention to your soul is even harder.

Simone Weil was an amazing French woman who had a dramatic conversion experience. She had a deep and profound appreciation for attentiveness, especially in prayer. She died in 1943 at the age of thirty-three but left a significant legacy. So much so that the French government issued a postage stamp in her honor. The stamp bears her image and is inscribed with the words "Attention is the only faculty of the soul which gives us access to God."[4]

You Have Control of Your Soul

So, as we think about our one and only life, we must learn to pay attention to our souls. And, as we do this, our lives will be healthier and richer.

Here's the good news. Having a great soul has nothing to do with how much you make, what you own, how you look, how skinny you are, or how much charisma you have. And here's more good news: you have far more control over your soul than you do over all the external pieces of your life. You don't have control over the economy or the stock market or the weather or your boss or other drivers or cancer. But you are 100 percent the gardener of your interior life. You have complete control over your anger, joy, gratitude, greed, passion, desires, spiritual vitality, and values.

In the Bible, God never gives anyone a cushy, comfortable, easy existence. No! Following God is demanding, challenging, daunting, and self-sacrificing. Jesus promised that in this world we would experience trouble. Every one of us could give testimony validating Jesus's prediction. The Bible does use the word *easy* once, though:

> Come to me, all you who are weary and burdened, and I will give you rest. Take my yoke upon you and learn from me, for I am gentle and humble in heart, and you will find rest for your souls. For my yoke is *easy* and my burden is light. (Matt. 11:28–30 NIV, emphasis added)

Notice that Jesus doesn't say life will be easy, He says His yoke is easy.

When we are yoked to Jesus and do life His way, it works. It doesn't have to be exhausting and depressing and soul-sucking. And it begins with learning to be the gardener of our own soul.

Contrary to what Elizabeth Hurley's character said, your soul is not like your appendix. It's much more like your heart. It's the center of your being.

So, how about you? Have you been living as though souls are overrated?

REFLECTION/DISCUSSION QUESTIONS

1. For you personally, what does it mean to be the gardener of your soul?

2. Explain what you think Simone Weil was getting at when she said, "Attention is the only faculty of the soul which gives us access to God."

3. How would you answer the question "How is it with your soul?"

4. Read Matthew 11:28–30 again but read it slowly. What stands out to you from these words of Jesus?

CHAPTER 7

What Story Are You Telling Yourself?

Be yourself. Everyone else is already taken.

RICHARD AND LEONA BERGSTROM

JUST BE YOURSELF. Three simple words. What could be easier? It sounds like the simplest of requests. It doesn't take a college degree or a certain level of IQ. It's not about skill or gifting. If there's anything that seems like it should come naturally for us, it is "being ourselves." And yet, truly learning how to be yourself is one of the most challenging undertakings of your life.

E. E. Cummings accurately said, "To be nobody-but-yourself in a world which is doing its best, night and day, to make you everybody else—means to fight the hardest battle which any human being can fight."[1]

From the moment you took your first breath, your sense of self was like a moist lump of clay. And every day the voices and experiences of your life have been shaping and forming your sense of self.

Criticisms, compliments, and conversations have been molding you since the first day you arrived on this planet.

It's not just coaches, teachers, parents, and friends who intentionally or unintentionally shape your sense of self. The entire culture is bombarding you with messages that challenge and manipulate your sense of self. Every single day there is an avalanche of advertisers trying to get you to believe your sense of self is connected to the car you drive, the vacation you take, or the pants you wear.

Subtle Self-Talk

Before long, we begin to see ourselves in a certain way, and that perception informs our self-talk. There emerges a story that we tell ourselves about our "self."

I'm a leader.
I don't belong.
I'm never quite good enough.
I can become anything I want.
I'm a disappointment to myself and others.
I can make a difference.
I'm not wanted.
I am loved.

Those phrases may not be your story, but I can promise there is a story you're telling yourself. That story is like an incredible torrent that runs deep beneath all the noise and busyness of your life. And it has incredible power in your life.

Our self-talk begins to shape how we see and interact with the world. There's a fascinating study called the Scar Experiment. A researcher secured ten volunteers to participate in the project. They were told that the purpose of the study was to observe how people would respond to a stranger with a marred physical appearance, such as a facial scar. Using professional Hollywood makeup artists, they applied a gruesome scar on each person's left cheek. Then, using a handheld mirror, they showed the scar to each participant. After that, they told each volunteer that they needed to apply some finishing powder to the scar. But in actuality, the makeup artists subtly removed the scar.

The volunteers were instructed to go out into the waiting rooms of the medical offices where they were conducting the experiment. They were to notice how strangers responded to their appearance. After a short time, the volunteers returned to the office. They reported that strangers were rude, unkind, and stared at their scar. Even though the fake scars had been removed, their self-perception affected how they thought others viewed them.[2]

The physical and/or emotional wounds and scars that we carry profoundly shape our sense of self and how we believe others see us. Even though deep down we may feel unacceptable, early in life we quickly learn how to play the game of getting acceptance. No matter what our sense of our internal, private self, we learn to project an outward, public self that is acceptable. It's how we learn to get along so that we can belong.

That has been my story. Somehow, very early in my life, the story I began to tell myself was that I wasn't enough. Even though I grew up in a very loving and affirming home, the story that I wasn't enough took root in my soul. Honestly, for many years I wasn't aware that was the story I was telling myself. But to compensate for that internal script, I put my ambition into overdrive. I worked hard to make good grades. I worked hard to excel in sports. I became president of my senior class. I graduated college early. I graduated seminary early. I even graduated from singleness early; I got married at the immature age of nineteen. The result was that I was compulsively busy and always trying to outrun my "not being enough."

In many respects, my ambition really served me well. It opened a lot of doors, and most people I know would have seen me as hardworking and successful. When you're a highly driven, workaholic overachiever, you get a lot of pats on the back. But here's the problem. Some of the things that people will applaud in your life will actually wreck your soul and your sense of "self." So, while all those pats on the back were salve on my "not-enoughness," they simply masked the deeper problem.

Judith Hougen nailed me when she wrote, "We feel pulled to produce, to perform, to plow through the next five things on the to-do list. This is the hand of the false self slowly, silently pushing us toward frenetic busyness. Our doing has become our being, and the untended garden of the inner life becomes overgrown with the tangled activities of an illusory person."[3]

The words that most grab me are "untended garden of the inner life." As we talked about in the last chapter, I was oblivious to the garden of my inner life (soul). I had never stopped long enough or been reflective enough to really examine why I was doing what I was doing. I was completely unaware of the internal drivers that kept pushing me. And I never questioned whether my ambition was healthy or godly.

Self-Reflection Leads to Self-Awareness

I have found it helpful and informative to stop long enough to reflect on the garden of my inner life. It's helpful to ponder the question "What is the story I'm constantly telling myself?" If you don't identify the narrative in your soul, you will focus only on managing the externals. And that is shortsighted.

Let me give you an example from my own journey. By nature, I am restless and really enjoy being active and getting things accomplished. This is, of course, connected to the narrative I've created. I have always been a student of personal productivity. Don't judge me, but I like reading books about time management. I'm always trying to figure out how to get more done in less time.

One day I was looking over my calendar and trying to figure out how to juggle some commitments to make room for some additional work I wanted to take on. Then, out of the blue, the Holy Spirit ambushed me. It was like the Spirit took the spotlight off my calendar and shined it on my soul. Internally, I began to hear questions like "Why are you so compulsively busy?" and "Why is your calendar constantly overcommitted?" Those were not time-management questions. They were soul questions. They were about the internal story that was driving me. God was moving the conversation from the external to the internal.

As long as we're simply managing the externals of our lives, we're signing up for a never-satisfying life of clawing, grabbing, striving, pushing, and chasing. It reminds me of young David, the shepherd boy, volunteering to fight Goliath, the Philistines' special forces soldier. If you remember the story, King Saul offers David his armor. It is bulky and cumbersome. It doesn't fit. It feels uncomfortable. It won't work. David is self-aware enough and wise enough to reject Saul's armor.

When we try to be somebody we were never meant to be or project a hologram in hopes we'll be liked and accepted, we are wearing somebody else's armor. In the long run, it doesn't work. Also, we'll always wonder whether people love the real us or simply the hologram we have projected.

By the way, this is the perfect recipe for the making of a Pharisee. When there's a division between what I project externally and who I really am, hypocrisy is lurking nearby.

False Self vs. True Self

In David Benner's book *The Gift of Being Yourself*, he talks about the false self and the true self. I have taken his list and adapted it. The entire left column is all about wearing Saul's armor.

False Self	True Self
1. Significance achieved by what we have, what we can do, and what others think of us	1. Significance achieved by being deeply loved by God
2. Happiness sought in autonomy from God and in attachments	2. Fulfillment found in surrender to God and living in our calling
3. Identity is our idealized self (who we want others to think we are)	3. Identity is who we are—and are becoming—in Christ

False Self	True Self
4. Achieved by means of pretense and performance	4. Received as a gift with gratitude and surrender
5. Maintained by effort and control	5. Maintained by grace
6. Duplicitous (image management)	6. Congruent (integrated)
7. Exhausting	7. Life-giving
8. Looks to people for validation	8. Looks to God for validation[4]

This is something I have been aware of and working on for the last several years, but it still can be an issue in my life. I remember a party we attended when I was well into my fifties and I had a false self (left column) moment.

There were probably a dozen or so people at the party, and several of the guys there were very sharp, intelligent, and articulate. To be honest, I felt a little intimidated. I kept trying to join in the conversation, but I felt out of place. Finally, one of the guys turned and said, "I want to know what you think." And I drew an absolute blank. I mumbled some lame answer. It was definitely not tweet worthy. Then the shame storm started brewing. *I'm such an idiot. My one moment to contribute to an intelligent conversation and I sounded like a bumbling fool.* I think most of us are way more fragile internally than we want others to believe.

The older I get, the more my deep desire is to live from the true self (right column). I want to shed Saul's armor. When Saul's armor has been your cover for years, it's not easy to break loose. But there is freedom in shedding the layers of the false self. There is joy in finally getting comfortable with who you are and who you aren't.

When you can live from a place of internal peace and deep acceptance of your true self, that is a gift. It's a gift to yourself, to your family and friends, and to the world.

This is beautifully put on display for us in the life of Jesus. Think for a moment about the times in Jesus's life when He heard

God's audible voice. The first time God is recorded to have spoken words out of heaven in the life of Jesus was at His baptism.

> After his baptism, as Jesus came up out of the water, the heavens were opened and he saw the Spirit of God descending like a dove and settling on him. And a voice from heaven said, "This is my dearly loved Son, who brings me great joy." (Matt. 3:16–17)

This is on the very front end of Jesus's ministry. He hadn't preached a sermon, cast out a demon, healed a blind man, or raised somebody from the dead. These words were spoken over His obscure and hidden years. They had nothing to do with His performance. They had to do with sonship. Author and speaker Alicia Britt Chole writes,

> Having fully captivated Jesus' and John's attention, of all the things Father God could have said, his first words were neither directional ("Go here") nor instructional ("Do this"). They were relational: "This is my son."[5]

In the journey of every mature Christ follower, a transformation has to take place. Instead of chasing after the approval and validation of others to find our identity and worth, we choose to rest in the fact that we are a child of God . . . and that is enough.

But it takes courage to no longer act externally in ways that are inconsistent with who we truly are internally. In other words, it takes guts to discard Saul's armor.

I love the words of Henri Nouwen when he says, "The change of which I speak is the change from living life as a painful test to prove that you deserve to be loved, to living it as an unceasing 'Yes' to the truth of that Belovedness."[6]

For some of us, our souls are worn out from living out of the false self. We're exhausted trying to find our significance in what we achieve. We are weary from lugging Saul's armor through life. We're burned out from trying to live somebody else's life. Right now . . . this moment . . . here and now could be a defining moment in your life. Make the courageous choice to truly be yourself and accept that you are God's beloved. Let those words of acceptance wash over your soul. It is very soothing and healing.

If you don't settle your identity issue, you'll settle for an unsettled life.

REFLECTION/DISCUSSION QUESTIONS

1. Who has been a powerful voice in your life that tried to shape your sense of "self"? It could be a coach, a relative, a friend, a teacher, a parent, or someone else.

2. What is the story (internal script) deeply entrenched in your soul that you have been telling yourself?

3. Look back over the false-self and true-self lists. From the false-self list, what is one item that you need to be most aware of? From the true-self list, what is one item that you most need to embrace?

4. Zephaniah 3:17 says,

> For the LORD your God is living among you.
>> He is a mighty savior.
> He will take delight in you with gladness.
>> With his love, he will calm all your fears.
>> He will rejoice over you with joyful songs.

When you read the words that God delights in you with gladness and rejoices over you with joyful songs, what do you think and feel?

CHAPTER 8

Is Self-Care Selfish?

> We don't forget that we are Christians. We forget
> that we are human, and that one oversight alone
> can debilitate the potential in our future.
>
> WAYNE CORDEIRO

SELF-CARE AND SELF-LEADERSHIP go hand in hand. In order for you to live the life you long for, you must learn how to appropriately care for yourself. One of the most important lessons I have been learning in the last few years is that self-care isn't selfish, it's good stewardship.

Earlier I mentioned verse 2 in 3 John. It's a rather obscure verse and one that I paid little attention to. But in recent years, it has become very meaningful to me. John writes, "Dear friend, I pray that you may enjoy good health and that all may go well with you, even as your soul is getting along well" (NIV).

John prays that those reading his letter would "enjoy good health." God not only wants you to experience good health but also wants you to actually "enjoy" it. In addition, John also prays that all will go well with these first-century Christ followers, even as their souls are getting along well. I don't think John is praying that everything in their lives will be easy and smooth. I think he is praying that they will experience a quality of life that will allow them to thrive, no matter what's going on around them.

Good health, a thriving soul, and a rich quality of life require a measure of self-care.

If I neglect caring for myself, doing things that fill my tank, and living within my limits, my soul will begin to shrivel.

In this day of obsession with the selfie, self-actualization, self-esteem, and self-indulgence, it's easy to become self-absorbed. There is certainly a line we can cross where our self-care becomes selfish.

Denying Self vs. Caring for Self

When Jesus talked about what it means to follow Him, He often spoke about denying self, forsaking self, and dying to self. At the heart of being an apprentice of Jesus is the idea of self-surrender. It's the idea of letting God and His truth rule my life, not my *self*ish desires. Surrender is the path to God's best for my life.

But denying self is not the same as self-loathing or self-hatred or self-neglect. We must remember that we are created in the image of God, and we are His image bearers. And while we have been marred by sin, that doesn't diminish our intrinsic value or worth. We've been endowed by God with a soul and a body. It's that soul and body (self) that is the vehicle through which we'll live our one and only life on this planet. A "self" that is surrendered to God is a beautiful thing meant to be cared for and appreciated.

So where is the line between self-care and self-absorption? That's a tricky question and one that you have to personally discern. I don't think there is an easy formula that applies to everyone. We're all unique, and self-care looks different for each of us.

However, I do think there are two key guiding thoughts that can help us in that discernment process. First, anything that falls under the rubric of self-care must be consistent with God's Word and the lifestyle of a follower of Jesus. You could not justify getting drunk as a means of self-care to temporarily escape your problems. The Bible is clear that a believer is not to get drunk. Whatever we do to care for ourselves must align with God's unchanging truth. Second, true self-care is a means to an end, not an end in itself.

Think of your personal self-care like maintenance for your car. When you take your car for an oil change, you don't sit in the waiting area and mutter to yourself, "You selfish car." You know that by stopping, pausing, and performing the needed maintenance, you're adding to the longevity and life of your vehicle. The same is true for your life. You might be so busy and your schedule so full that you don't think you have time to change the oil. You could get by with this for a little while, but if you neglect changing your oil, eventually it will have catastrophic consequences.

No one would ever accuse Jesus of being self-absorbed, but He did practice self-care. In Mark 6:30–31, we read, "The apostles returned to Jesus from their ministry tour and told him all they had done and taught. Then Jesus said, 'Let's go off by ourselves to a quiet place and rest awhile.' He said this because there were so many people coming and going that Jesus and his apostles didn't even have time to eat."

I love that Jesus is concerned for the well-being of the disciples. They were obviously depleted from a busy season of ministry. It was not selfish that they needed to rest and replenish. It was not selfish that they needed to take a break so they could eat and refuel their bodies. This was about the need for physical self-care. But there is also a need for spiritual self-care.

In Luke 5:15–16, we read, "But despite Jesus' instructions, the report of his power spread even faster, and vast crowds came to hear him preach and to be healed of their diseases. But Jesus often withdrew to the wilderness for prayer." In the life of Jesus, there was the constant pressure of people's needs coming at Him. Notice that the passage says "vast crowds" were coming to Him. Jesus certainly could have stayed at it until every person was healed and every need was met. But He didn't. In this passage, He modeled for us a very important truth. There will always be more work that could be done and more needs that could be met. But those who practice good self-care know that you must stop and change the oil and fill up the tank with fuel.

Running on Empty

I can tell you from personal experience that trying to do life on "empty" is a miserable place to live. It leads to burnout, cynicism, frustration, and resentment.

Another great example comes from the life of Elijah. In 1 Kings 18, Elijah experiences a spiritual high that is both exhilarating and exhausting. If you're not familiar with Elijah's encounter with the prophets of Baal, you should definitely read it.

Right after this epic event, Elijah prays seven times for rain that will break the famine. God answers his prayer and is about to send a "gullywasher." (If you don't know what a gullywasher is, ask someone from the South.) Then 1 Kings 18:46 says, "Then the LORD gave special strength to Elijah. He tucked his cloak into his belt and ran ahead of Ahab's chariot all the way to the entrance of Jezreel."

Elijah runs a distance just short of a marathon. He runs twenty-five miles and outruns Ahab's chariot. For a preacher, that is impressive!

When he gets to Jezreel, he receives word from Jezebel that within twenty-four hours she will kill him. Elijah had single-handedly just confronted hundreds of Baal's prophets. Surely, he would be unfazed by one evil woman. What we read next is stunning:

> Elijah was afraid and fled for his life. He went to Beersheba, a town in Judah, and he left his servant there. Then he went on alone into the wilderness, traveling all day. He sat down under a solitary broom tree and prayed that he might die. "I have had enough, LORD," he said. "Take my life, for I am no better than my ancestors who have already died." (1 Kings 19:3–4)

What happened to this fearless prophet of God? He's empty. He doesn't have anything left in the tank. Exhaustion makes cowards of us all. Great highs are often followed by great lows. Often, moments of victory are moments of intensity; we have expended all of our energy, and we can feel drained.

You see, Elijah was bumping up against his limits. After six decades of living, I am finally beginning to embrace the fact that I have limits. And those limits are a gift from God. As Geri Scazzero says in her book *I Quit*, "I did not understand the powerful, biblical principle of limits as a gift from the hand of God. God places boundaries around every living thing, including human beings. . . . We have limits specific to our age, personality, marital status, children, gifts, education, family of origin, and economic status."[1]

Also notice that Elijah's exhaustion skews his perspective. He's ready to die. All he can see in this moment is the negative. When you're empty, often the story you tell yourself is one that exaggerates and magnifies your problems.

Here are some other warning signs that you might not be doing a great job of self-care:

- You constantly feel exhausted.
- You feel emotionally numb.
- You've lost the ability to have fun.
- You act as though you don't have limits.
- You think you are the exception . . . and the rules don't apply to you.
- You find yourself irritable and have to fight off explosions of anger.
- All you want to do is escape.
- You waste hours and hours binge-watching mindless television.
- You don't do anything that is consistently life-giving.
- You're self-medicating instead of self-caring.

It's interesting to see how God responds to Elijah in this situation. I love that God doesn't chastise Elijah. He doesn't scold him or tell him to "suck it up and get back to work." He doesn't lecture him and tell him to change his attitude. No! He lets Elijah sleep and then has an angel bring him food. After eating, Elijah takes another nap and then eats some more.

Give It a Rest

Sometimes the most spiritual thing you can do is take a nap and enjoy a good meal. Psalm 127:2 says that "God gives rest to his loved ones."

During my years at Saddleback Church, I served as an executive pastor and teaching pastor. I did a terrible job of self-care. I worked all the time. I thought being "all in" meant going all out all the time. My soul paid a price, my friends paid a price, and my family definitely paid a price. I failed to find a balance between serving others and honoring my own needs and desires.

I didn't have any healthy hobbies and lost any desire for recreation. When someone would invite me to play golf or go for a bike ride, my first thought was about how much work I could get done in the time it would take to do something recreational.

What I didn't realize at the time is that self-care is not only a gift to yourself but also to those around you. When you're healthy and replenished and your tank is filled, you're a better person and a lot more fun to be around.

I remember sitting in a room one day with about three hundred church leaders. The guest speaker said a lot of great things that day, but one illustration he used reached out and grabbed me by the throat. When you're born, he said, God gives you a palette of colors with which to paint a beautiful life. "My problem with most of you in this room is that you only paint with the ministry color." *Ouch!* He was spot-on. Yes, our work matters. But God has also given us five senses and a great big world to explore and experience and *enjoy*.

So, how about it? What steps do you need to take to better care for yourself?

- ▸ Get more sleep
- ▸ Eat healthier

- Exercise
- Practice Sabbath
- Take up a hobby or sport
- Take control of your electronic devices
- Pursue a new friendship
- Schedule your vacations for the year
- Schedule a personal retreat for prayer, solitude, and think time
- Get outside and enjoy creation
- Plan a getaway with your spouse

In order to do self-care properly, we'll need to be reflective and discerning about the things we truly value. We'll have to be self-aware about the activities and practices that fill our souls and make us better. We'll need to ponder the things that bring us true delight.

Take a few moments to complete the following exercise. Think about five things that fill your tank when you do them. List them in the Tank Filler spaces below.

Then, in the How Often section, list how frequently you need or want this activity, ideally. Is it daily, weekly, two times a month? Finally, in the Current Status space, rank the item on a scale of 1–10 for how well you're making time for it currently (1 = it's nonexistent in my life today, and 10 = I'm doing this consistently and it is life-giving to me).

Tank Filler	How Often	Current Status
1.		
2.		

Tank Filler	How Often	Current Status
3.		
4.		
5.		

Consider having a conversation with your spouse or a good friend about this. Discuss what practical steps you could take to better practice self-care. Then create and execute a plan. You'll be glad you did (and so will everyone else).

Remember, good self-care is not selfish, it is good stewardship of your one life.

REFLECTION/DISCUSSION QUESTIONS

1. What is one area where you're doing well with self-care? What is one area where you need to do a better job with self-care?

2. What is the single most important thing you need to do in order to keep your tank filled?

3. What are some of the warning signs you notice when you are not doing a good job of self-care?

4. What does it look like practically for you to live within your limits?

CHAPTER 9

Techno-Soul

What's the single biggest factor shaping
our lives today? *Our screens.*

ADAM ALTER

NEURONS THAT FIRE TOGETHER wire together. Those six words have huge implications for the health of your soul and the quality of your one and only life. That well-known statement among neuroscientists describes what happens as a result of our constant engagement with technology. Over time, your brain literally gets reprogrammed, and the results are staggering.

We all sense it and feel it. I feel it when I try to read my Bible. I feel it when I reflexively reach for my phone anytime I have a few spare seconds. I feel it when I'm supposed to be having a conversation with my wife and my head is buried in my computer. I feel it when I have a Pavlovian response to a new text message coming in.

In Palo Alto, California, a seventeen-year-old broke into a home in the middle of the night. That isn't uncommon. What is highly uncommon is why he broke into a complete stranger's house. He woke the sleeping homeowners, asking if he could use their Wi-Fi network because he had used all of his cellular data for the month.[1]

While we chuckle at this story, we all know the feeling of panic when we can't find our phone or our battery shows 1 percent.

Reality Check

The speed at which technology is advancing and invading our lives is mind-blowing. An article I read captured the acceleration of technology that we're watching unfold.

In 1958, a scientist at Texas Instruments developed the first-ever integrated circuit. It had two transistors (the more, the better) with a "gate process length" (the smaller, the better) of about half an inch. Fast-forward to 1971 to a processor developed by Intel. The Intel 4004 had 2,300 transistors with a gate length of 10,000 nanometers. By the way, a nanometer is one billionth of a meter. To give you a frame of reference, a sheet of paper is about 100,000 nanometers thick.

Now fast-forward another forty years to 2012. Nvidia released a new graphical processor unit (GPU) with 7.1 billion transistors and a gate length of 28 nanometers. You may have heard of the law of diminishing returns; this advancement in technology is now being called the law of accelerating returns. We're using faster tools to design and build faster tools. Ray Kurzweil's conclusion is that "we won't experience 100 years of progress in the 21st century—it will be more like 20,000 years of progress."[2]

And we all know that we are not going back to a quieter, slower, *simpler* time.

To get a grasp of the choke hold that technology has on our lives, consider the following data.

The average American

- ▸ spends eight hours a day staring at some kind of screen,
- ▸ is on social media two hours per day,

- checks their phone eighty-five times a day, and
- will spend two years of their life on Facebook.[3]

A 2015 study by Common Sense Media found that teenagers were consuming media—including text messaging and social networks—nine hours per day on average.[4]

Every single minute on the planet, YouTube users upload four hundred hours of video, and every day there are literally billions of Facebook "likes."[5]

It's hard to believe that the internet has only been around since about 1990.

Don't get me wrong, I love living in the age of technology. I love gadgets. I love being able to communicate by email. I love being able to FaceTime my granddaughters. I love apps that help me organize my world. I love being able to bank online. I love being able to use Google Maps to get where I want to go.

But I need to stare in the face the fact that the implications of technology on my soul are profound. Having a soul that's at peace and in deep union with Jesus requires space and quiet and stillness. Having a soul that knows how to deeply connect with others requires "presence" and attention. And our gadgets fight to consume every morsel of time and attention in our lives. They leave us with souls that are fatigued and fragmented. It's time for us to take back our lives.

Simply put, humans are not wired to be constantly wired.[6]

How Did We Get Here?

In most discussions about technology, the focus is on the content—the information and sounds and words and images that the technology delivers. The medium itself tends to fade into the background and center stage goes to the sizzle of everything this new, whiz-bang gadget can deliver.

But Marshall McLuhan warns us not to minimize the impact of the technology itself. He said, "The medium is the message."[7]

What's amazing about that statement is that McLuhan wrote it in 1964. This kind of prophetic statement made more than a half century ago is now being validated by neuroscience. It's the medium itself that is the biggest game changer.

A new technology does not add or subtract something. It changes everything. In the year 1500, fifty years after the printing press was invented, we did not have an old Europe plus the printing press. We had a different Europe.[8]

The years 1440 and 2007. Two significant years in the development of game-changing technologies. Johannes Gutenberg and Steve Jobs. Two significant people who unleashed two game-changing technologies. The printing press and the iPhone. Two technologies that forever changed the planet.

McLuhan works from the premise that "we become what we behold" and "we shape our tools and then our tools shape us."[9] When modern technology first appeared on the scene, it was like a tame, docile horse standing in the stable. We walked up to the horse, put one foot in the stirrup, and hoisted ourselves into the saddle. We were in control. We had a firm grip on the reins and began to slowly walk the horse around the stable. The ride was fun, intriguing, and safe.

The horse that we thought was tame is in fact a wild stallion. And the horse has broken out of the stable and is now running at a full gallop. We have fallen out of the saddle but still have one foot in the stirrup, and the horse is now in control, dragging us where he wants to take us.

We're finally beginning to understand that our devices are not innocuous. They have huge implications for the health of our souls and our lives. To really live the life we long to live, we must realize there's a dangerous downside to technology and get back in the saddle and take control.

We could spend this chapter detailing a long list of steps you could take to better manage all your devices. But what I'm advocating for is not a list of minor tweaks or helpful tips or internet filters. I want to challenge you with the bigger issue. As Cal Newport says in *Digital Minimalism*, you need "a full-fledged philosophy of technology use, rooted in your deep values."[10]

For example, if we value deep relationships, then paying attention is critical to facilitating those deep relationships. And when it comes to our devices, our attention is up for grabs. Our nervous twitch to constantly engage our devices has shattered our attention into a million little pieces . . . and all the king's horses and all the king's men can't seem to put us back together again.

The truth is, I am finding it increasingly difficult to focus on a task, pay attention for very long, be present in a conversation, have undistracted thoughts, pray without distraction, read deeply, enjoy a quiet drive, or be alone with my thoughts. When I step back, unplug for a few moments, and soberly reflect, I find I don't like what constant engagement with technology does to me.

What I am up against is something that's now labeled the "attention economy." Former Google designer Tristan Harris calls it an arms race for people's attention. A company gets paid by successfully keeping your attention on your device. When it comes to Facebook, you are not the client. Advertisers are the true clients. You, my friend, are the product. It's the precious seconds of your attention that are for sale.

Harris said, "If I'm Facebook or I'm Netflix or I'm Snapchat, I have literally a thousand engineers whose job is to get more attention from you. . . . The CEO of Netflix recently said our biggest competitors are Facebook, YouTube, and sleep."[11]

Microsoft researcher Linda Stone said that "continuous partial attention" is our new normal.[12]

There is no denying that we've all been deeply impacted by the advent of technology. It's not an exaggeration to say that technology is literally reshaping how we do life. Every minute I'm browsing the internet is a minute I am not engaged in a human encounter. Every hour spent on YouTube is an hour spent not enjoying the outdoors. It's all about what you truly value and what gives your life richness and meaning.

Take Back Control

So how do we take the control of our lives back from technology? How we steward our attention is the key.

Pay Attention to Your Attention

You are where your attention is. We're losing the ability to be quiet and alone with just our thoughts. We have an attraction to distraction. The tsunami of noise and information coming at us makes it hard to concentrate on anything for very long.

It was a bitterly cold morning in Denver. I boarded the Canopy Shuttle about 6:00 a.m. for my ten-minute ride to the airport terminal. I'd done this drill a thousand times. But I had already decided ahead of time this ride was going to be different. There were nine other bleary-eyed people joining me on the short journey. As we pulled onto Tower Road, the shuttle was dead silent. As you would expect, every person had their head buried in their smartphone. And that's where the experiment began. I had an increasing awareness that I was constantly plugged in and that my smartphone had become another appendage. I needed to learn to better manage the techno-gadgets in my life.

So I decided to try a little experiment. On that snowy morning, as I boarded the shuttle, I slid the phone into my jacket pocket. As we headed toward the airport, I enjoyed taking in the beauty of the snowcapped Rockies. I prayed some, thought about my upcoming trip, and just sat in silence with my thoughts. But that still left me with nine and a half minutes to go. It was way harder for me to go ten minutes without looking at my phone than I would want you to know. At least six or seven times during that short ride I reflexively reached for my phone, because that's what I do whenever I have a few spare seconds.

I can relate to Nicholas Carr's words in his book *The Shallows*: "In the choices we have made, consciously or not, about how we use our computers, we have rejected the intellectual tradition of solitary, single-minded concentration."[13]

Our incessant screen time is causing an erosion in our ability to focus, concentrate, think, or reflect. Neuroscientists tell us that we don't read deeply and thoughtfully anymore. We just scan and decode information.

Pay Attention to Your God

The eight words and twenty-four letters of Psalm 46:10 are a huge indictment against modern Christ followers. BE. STILL. AND. KNOW. THAT. I. AM. GOD.

If being still is a requisite for knowing God, no wonder we have trouble with spiritual practices like prayer, solitude, meditation, and silence. I get to do a lot of life coaching with Christian leaders, and when I begin to probe around on their spiritual life, I uncover a common theme. Most all of these people are regularly spending time in God's Word, but they struggle to pay attention and focus. We're constantly tempted to check our email, Facebook, Twitter, and newsfeeds.

It's been helpful for me to put my phone out of arm's reach when I'm trying to read my Bible, pray, or practice silence. Let's connect this back to the issue of my values. If I truly value a deep and intimate relationship with God, then I'm going to need to have technology practices and boundaries that actually protect that value.

I also find this is an issue when I attend church. I stopped bringing my Bible to church and started carrying my iPad because it was lighter and just more convenient. After all, I had YouVersion readily available. But after a few weeks, I noticed that I was having a hard time staying fully engaged in the service. I found myself distracted by a variety of things on my iPad that kept calling my name. So, if I truly value connecting with God during a church service, then I may need to go "old school" and carry my Bible instead of my iPad.

Pay Attention to Your Relationships

Here's a principle that would be good for us to adopt: don't be distracted from the person who is there by the person who isn't there. As you read the Gospels, you can see that Jesus never seems to be distracted, preoccupied, or checked out when He is with someone. They always seem to have His full attention.

In her book *Reclaiming Conversation*, Sherry Turkle says, "Face-to-face conversation is the most human—and humanizing—thing we do. Fully present to one another, we learn to listen. It's where we develop the capacity for empathy. It's where we experience the joy of being heard, of being understood."[14]

So could I challenge you to put your smartphone down and take a step back? Give these questions some serious thought. What do you seriously value and hold dear in your life? As you think about your one and only life, what is it that you cherish and that gives you deep joy? What is it that you want to fill your days?

Finally, ponder these words from Christi Straub: "Look back at your life this past week and tell me about the moments that mattered. The ones that made you feel real joy, belly laugh, and take a deep breath of thankfulness. The moments you'll remember ten years from now. I doubt any of them happened on a screen."[15]

REFLECTION/DISCUSSION QUESTIONS

1. As you think about your own use of technology, what is one behavior or pattern that can be unhealthy?

2. How can technology become a barrier to one of your personal values?

3. How do you think technology has impacted your relationship with God?

4. What is one step you can take with your devices that would help you have better relationships?

CHAPTER

10

You Owe Me

Blessed is he who expects nothing,
for he shall enjoy everything.

ST. FRANCIS OF ASSISI

ST. FRANCIS OBVIOUSLY didn't live in the twenty-first century.
If we were to rewrite Francis's words to be a little more culturally
relevant, we might say, "Blessed is he who expects and demands
everything, for he shall enjoy what he has coming to him."

That prevalent cultural mindset can be summarized in one
word: *entitlement*. Entitlement will poison your one and only life
and rob you of contentment, gratitude, and joy. A few years ago, I
saw an interview with a young man who could have been the poster
child for entitlement. The interview took place during the Occupy
Wall Street movement. These protests against financial inequal-
ity took place in New York City's Wall Street financial district.
One college-age student was holding a sign that said, "Pay for my
tuition." A media reporter asked, "Why should the government
pay for your tuition?" The student answered, "Because they have
money, and I deserve a free college education."[1] I'm sure that was
a proud moment for his parents.

John Townsend, in his book *The Entitlement Cure*, defines *entitlement* as the "belief that I am exempt from responsibility and I am owed special treatment."[2]

The *Cambridge Dictionary* provides an even more colorful definition of *entitlement*. It is "the feeling that you have the right to do or have what you want without having to work for it or deserve it, just because of who you are."[3]

A Look in the Mirror

Before we look down our noses with disgust at those "self-absorbed ingrates," it might be good for us to take a look at the subtle ways that entitlement has invaded our own hearts.

I am definitely not writing as someone who has conquered this devious sin in my life. Part of what makes this hard to write about is that I know entitlement has more of a stranglehold on me than I want to admit. And it can be ugly. Even after following Jesus for more than a half century, it's still a daily battle.

One of the places entitlement shows up in my life is in the area of travel. As a consultant, I travel a lot, and travel can breed entitlement. The airline industry builds loyalty with status and keeping score. The way you keep score is with miles, and miles buy you status and privilege (which is fuel for entitlement). When you have status, you get your own check-in line. You get a little tag that gives your bag priority. (So even my luggage has entitlement issues.) You board before other people, you get to place your bags in the overhead bins before other people, and you deplane before other people. And if you're fortunate enough to get an upgrade to first class, not only do you get a larger seat, but you get a hot towel to wipe your face and you also get actual food.

Then, here's what happens: when you don't get upgraded or when you don't get a hot towel and you have to wipe your face on your neighbor's sleeve or you have to pay to watch TV, you feel slighted. I can begin to feel like United Airlines owes me an upgrade. After all, I spend a lot of money with them. I *deserve* my upgrade.

But keeping score doesn't just happen in the travel industry; it can happen anywhere. It can worm its way into your thoughts and dramatically impact how you approach life, how you function on your team, and how you relate to your family. It can even shape how you view your relationship with God.

My sin nature and selfish tendencies make the battle against entitlement intense. Remember from our last chapter that there is a difference between healthy self-care and unhealthy self-absorption.

A Look out the Window

But the battle against entitlement isn't just internal. There are some external cultural realities that make this battle doubly hard.

First, we live in a culture obsessed with self-esteem. Teaching kids they are the center of the universe only reinforces entitlement. We now live in a culture where some parents constantly tell their kids how special they are and most often side with their kids over teachers. Kids get a trophy for just showing up. No wonder so many kids are growing up with an attitude that the world owes them.

We seem to have forgotten that children are born with a selfish sin nature, and the sin nature naturally moves toward entitlement. The book of Proverbs says that "folly is bound up in the heart of a child" (22:15 NIV).

When I was an executive pastor at Saddleback Church, one weekend we had a group of five Buddhist priests from Japan who came to visit our services. I was one of the pastors assigned to host them on Saturday night. After they had attended the Saturday afternoon service, we had a time to sit with them and debrief their experience at an evangelical church. It was a fascinating conversation. At one point, one of the priests said, "The most difficult thing for me to accept about Christian belief is the belief in a sin nature. I just don't get it." In that moment, I remember thinking to myself, *That is one of the easiest for me to believe!*

Just look at every two-year-old you know. You don't have to teach them to be selfish or to lie or to fight or to throw a fit when they don't get their way. No, they come factory-installed with a sin nature.

That's why entitlement comes so easy. It's natural and reflective of our sin nature.

Second, we live in a culture of "handouts." We now live in a generation where people can get benefits without the responsibility of work. If we're poor, we deserve help from the government; if we're rich, we deserve a tax break; if we're a bank, we deserve a bailout; if we're a farm operation, we deserve subsidies.

I'm all for being compassionate and helping those in true need. That's not what I'm referring to. What I'm talking about is an attitude that expects a handout even when we're capable of taking responsibility and working to provide for ourselves.

Third, we live in a day of pervasive marketing and consumerism. A huge portion of our economy is built on stimulating dissatisfaction in us. Billions of dollars are spent on marketing campaigns to get us to focus on what we don't have rather than simply being grateful for what we do have. Advertisers are not content until we are discontent.

Marketing breeds in us the belief that we are entitled to a better car, a new iPad, or an exotic vacation. Advertising constantly stirs these desires in us. Consumerism isn't the same as entitlement, but it isn't a big leap from consumerism to entitlement.

And we would be naïve to think that the poisons of obsession with self-esteem, a culture of handouts, and pervasive consumerism haven't gotten into our bloodstream. None of us is exempt. Entitlement is one of those qualities that's easy to recognize in others but not so easy to recognize in ourselves. And when we do see it in others, it's always repulsive. I have never been drawn to someone with a spirit of entitlement. You will never see entitlement on a list of core values.

The Great Battle of Discipleship

So what does the Bible say about entitlement? Well, you won't ever read the word *entitlement* in the Bible, but the issue is addressed countless times. In Luke 9:23, Jesus said, "Whoever wants to be my disciple must deny themselves and take up their cross daily and follow me" (NIV).

Crushing entitlement is at the heart of discipleship. Entitlement says, "It's all about me and what I want and think I deserve." The primary battle in discipleship is the battle of self. The issue is whether Jesus will sit on the throne or whether "self" will sit on the throne. At its core, followership of Jesus is about dying to self and laying down my rights.

When speaking of Jesus, the apostle Paul gives us the most powerful anti-entitlement verses in all of Scripture.

> Though he was God,
>   he did not think of equality with God
>   as something to cling to.
> Instead, he gave up his divine privileges;
>   he took the humble position of a slave
>   and was born as a human being. (Phil. 2:6–7)

I am never less like Jesus than when I evidence a spirit of entitlement.

Entitlement manifests itself in words and actions, but the real battleground is a mindset, a way of thinking. The Bible names followers of Jesus as both slaves and sons/daughters. These two descriptors can feel contradictory. But both labels are used over and over to describe our relationship with Jesus. Our biblical understanding of our identity doesn't emphasize one over the other. I think the proper response is to embrace the tension of being both a slave and a son/daughter. By now, you're probably asking yourself, "What does this have to do with the topic of entitlement?" Well, I'm so glad you asked.

I believe your mindset about slavery and sonship has everything to do with entitlement. If you start with the mindset that we are slaves who have been given the unbelievable blessing of sonship, that fuels gratitude and crushes entitlement. But if you start with the mindset that you are a privileged child who has been given the unpleasant burden of servitude, that way of thinking breeds entitlement.

The Antidote to Entitlement

In this day when entitlement seduces us at every turn, what are some practical steps we can take to resist it?

1. *Choose a different mindset.* As we talked about earlier, each one of us has a God-given "decider." I get to choose my attitude and mindset. The diagram below reflects two very different mindsets.

I Deserve	I Am Responsible
Looks outward	Looks inward
Passive	Active
Others "owe" me	Jesus "owns" me
Victim	Overcomer
Unhealthy dependence	Healthy interdependence
Immaturity	Maturity
Looks for a handout	Looks for a solution
Taker	Contributor

2. *Stop blaming and start owning.* When you struggle with entitlement, all your discontentment is focused outward. They didn't come through for me. They let me down. They didn't meet my expectations.

   Wherever entitlement exists, blaming and whining will not be far behind. This issue is as old as the human race. When God asked Adam why he ate the forbidden fruit, Adam was quick to throw Eve under the bus. Being a quick study, when God asked Eve why she had eaten of the fruit, she pointed the finger of blame at the wily serpent. A sign of maturity is that I outwardly stop pointing the finger of blame and inwardly start taking responsibility.

3. *Pass the small daily tests.* You build your anti-entitlement muscles by passing the little daily tests that come your way. One might be a meeting you didn't get invited to, or it could be someone taking the parking space you were about to pull into. It could be a poor customer service experience or someone getting a nicer workspace than you. It could be getting passed over for a raise you thought you deserved, or it might be not getting from your spouse what you expect. I know that my bent toward entitlement will get tested several times a day and that it's good for my growth and character to regularly give up what I think are my rights.

4. *Practice generosity.* The antidote to the poison of entitlement is generosity. Pick something from the following list and commit to do it this week.

   ▸ Give away a prized possession.

   ▸ Lavishly serve a friend or family member without expecting anything in return.

   ▸ Anonymously bless a neighbor.

   ▸ Make a list of one hundred things you're grateful for.

   ▸ Read and meditate on Luke 17:7–10. You've probably never heard a sermon on this passage before.

   ▸ Encourage and celebrate something good that happened to somebody in your world.

   ▸ Read and reflect on Philippians 2:5–8. Then identify one privilege that you could give up to make sure entitlement is kept at bay.

   Before you move on with your day, I want to ask you to sit quietly for a few moments with the following question.

Where does entitlement show up in your attitudes and actions? Ask the Holy Spirit to shine the spotlight on anything that might resemble entitlement.

REFLECTION/DISCUSSION QUESTIONS

1. Earlier in this chapter I said, "Consumerism isn't the same as entitlement, but it isn't a big leap from consumerism to entitlement." How do marketing and consumerism feed into a spirit of entitlement?

2. From the I Deserve and I Am Responsible lists, circle an item from each column that most stands out to you. Why did you circle those particular words?

3. Where can entitlement worm its way into your thinking? As you think about your daily life, where could entitlement be a temptation?

4. In this chapter, I challenged you to use generosity as the antidote to entitlement. Either from the list I provided or an idea you have, what will you commit to do this week that will demonstrate generosity and keep entitlement at bay?

Part 3

IT'S ABOUT TIME!

11

What's the Big Hurry?

Hurry is the great enemy of spiritual life in our day.
You must ruthlessly eliminate hurry from your life.

DALLAS WILLARD

COVID-19. It changed our world. It changed my world. Who would have ever thought that a microscopic virus could bring the entire planet to its knees. As I sit down to write this chapter, we're right in the throes of the coronavirus pandemic. Right now it feels like the only thing we know with certainty . . . is there is global uncertainty. I hope by the time you read these words, life has returned to some sense of normalcy. But who knows what the "new normal" will look like and how long it will take to get there. By the time you read this, one thing I am confident of is that people will still be using the stockpile of toilet paper they purchased during the pandemic. After our last visit to the store to stockpile toilet paper and coffee (life's two most essential resources), I told my wife that our credit cards were now under orders to shelter at home.

The coronavirus forced planet Earth into an involuntary time-out. We were forced to stop going to restaurants and sporting events and concerts and schools and churches. Most of our nation was placed under orders to shelter at home, which is code for don't go anywhere.

I have a strong sense that once the restrictions are lifted and people feel safe to venture out, it won't be long until we're all living at an insane pace again. We'll once again begin to complain about our overscheduled lives, relentless demands, compulsive busyness, and pervasive exhaustion. I get it. By nature, I am an active person, and I like it that way. I like being busy. I'm driven. I obsess about managing my time well. I have a long history of filling up my calendar and then complaining about the hassle of an overcommitted schedule. I have a hard time sitting for very long, and my wife has told me for forty-plus years that I don't know how to relax. Somewhere along the journey of life I picked up a lie that got deeply embedded in my mind. The lie said, "Busy people are important people. So, if you want to be important, you better be busy." In case you haven't figured it out by now, I have issues!

To further complicate things, everything in our culture seems to be about going faster and getting everything done quicker. Life is open for business 24/7. There's not much about modern culture that is friendly to slowing down.

The truth is, outside of a government order to shelter at home, we find it very difficult to slow down. Let's face it: we're intoxicated with speed. My wife and I have been watching a Netflix series about Formula 1 racing called *The Drive to Survive*. I had no clue about the kind of money spent on a Formula 1 racing car. The top teams have several hundred employees and an annual budget north of $500 million. And it is all dedicated to creating a car that can run over 200 mph in a race that's less than 200 miles in length. I must admit, I would love to attend an F1 race. What a rush! There is also an adrenaline rush that comes with a fast-paced life.

In spite of the hundreds of millions spent, these finely tuned F1 cars often have problems. The tires begin to wear unevenly, the brakes begin to malfunction, the gearbox goes out, the engine overheats, or there's a loss of power. And then there's the problem of running into other cars or hitting the wall. One thing I noticed from watching the series is that going fast can cause you to crash. You can just call me Captain Obvious.

Take Your Foot Off the Accelerator

I don't know about you, but there's something deep in my soul that really does long for a life that's more simple and less frantic. I don't want to miss out on the stuff that's most important because I'm always in a hurry. Brendon Burchard describes what we all feel:

> We have stopped sensing the stillness, the stunning fullness and beauty and divine perfection of the moment. Most barrel through life, unaware of their senses and surroundings, deaf and blind to the magic of . . . this . . . very . . . moment. We are not supposed to miss it all, this life, but we do, all frazzled, stressed, and stripped away from Now. The cost is immense—so many moments blurred by speed and worry and panic, all stacking onto hectic days, all creating the catastrophe of an un-experienced, joyless life.[1]

If I'm being totally transparent, I have some regrets of things I missed because of my compulsive busyness and relentless hurry. But in recent years I've been on a path to detox from an addiction to speed and hurry. I like the trajectory of my life these days, and I can feel my soul coming alive. As I've been doing some of the hard, internal, reflective soul work, I am learning to slow down. I'm finally facing head-on some of the broken stuff in me that drives me in unhealthy ways. I'm learning to be more present. My internal rpms are not constantly redlining. It feels good!

I have a friend who was diagnosed with a precancerous tumor. It was serious enough that his colon was removed, and he went through a few months of treatment. It was definitely a defining moment in his life. As a result, he was forced to take a leave of absence, and I helped fill in the gap while he was out. When it was time for him to return to his ministry, he and I went to lunch together.

I was anxious to ask him a question. After just catching up and chitchatting for a while, I said, "So, you just went through a life-changing event, and you've had lots of time to think and reflect; what did God show you during your time away?"

With no hesitation whatsoever, he fired back, "Hurry destroys relationships." Let his words soak in for a moment. HURRY. DESTROYS. RELATIONSHIPS.

Constant busyness causes the heart and soul to harden and shrivel, and ultimately robs us of intimacy. This is true in our relationships with our kids, our friends, our spouse, and certainly with God.

As John Mark Comer says, "Hurry and love are incompatible. All my worst moments as a father, a husband, and a pastor, even as a human being, are when I'm in a hurry. . . . Hurry and love are oil and water: they simply do not mix."[2]

You can't live life at warp speed without warping your soul. An overcommitted schedule will lead to an undernourished soul. Let me say it more plainly: you can't follow Jesus at a sprint. To walk with God, you must go at a walking pace.[3]

It's interesting to me that when I read the Gospels, Jesus never seems rushed, frantic, hurried, or frazzled. He never seems distracted, preoccupied, or looking past a person to the next opportunity. One day Dallas Willard was asked what one word he would use to describe Jesus. His answer? "Relaxed."[4]

Don't let Willard's assessment paint a faulty picture in your mind of Jesus's life. You might be tempted to conclude that Jesus lived a nice, simple, easygoing, nondemanding life. The Gospels reveal a different picture. There were relentless demands, pressures, and opposition. He was run out of town, misunderstood, mocked, and ridiculed. And the religious leaders were constantly plotting ways to have Him killed. Jesus was fully engaged in the messiness of life, but He was unhurried and undistracted.

Just as it was true for Jesus, space and slowness are friends to our health: physical, emotional, relational, and spiritual. To really live the life we want, I believe most of us need increased space and a decreased pace. Busyness isn't just about an overcrowded calendar and too many self-inflicted commitments. It's also about filling every moment with noise and meaningless distraction. We must be rigorous to create space where we can reflect, think, listen, process, meditate . . . and just *be*.

A Tweak Won't Do It

I doubt there are many people who will read this chapter and disagree with my assessment of our lives and culture. We see it and feel it in our kids' schedules, in the accelerating pace of work life, in our impatience with our spouse, in how we do church, in our inability to detach from our smartphones, in our exhaustion as we collapse into bed, and in how we walk through a parking lot. Hurry and busyness are a thing.

I think where most of us struggle is in knowing how to actually make a change. I think most of us have resigned ourselves to the belief that "that's just the way it is and it's not gonna change." In the river of modern life, the fast current is just too strong, and we get swept along. I know what I'm advocating in this chapter is countercultural. But it seems that the Jesus way is always countercultural. I have a growing conviction about this: you won't tweak your way to a different reality. You have to make a dramatic shift. In order to slow the spread of the coronavirus, the world had to take radical steps. We implemented social distancing and sheltered at home and closed restaurants and playgrounds. Busyness likewise is a contagion that requires radical measures to eliminate.

You will probably need to have a "come to Jesus" meeting with your family. You will have to talk about ways to make some radical adjustments. You very well might need to alter your lifestyle. And you will have to be okay with letting some people down. Not everyone will be happy that you're taking greater control of your time. You'll have to stop believing the lie that what makes you important is how busy you are.

As I wrap up this chapter, I want to give you three highly practical steps you can begin to implement today.

Grab Your Calendar by the Throat

Your calendar is where your time and your values converge. Show me where your time goes and I'll tell you what you truly value. Many of us have what I call a theology of availability. Whatever people ask of us, the answer is yes.

We would never think of leaving our wallet out on the table and telling people to take whatever they need. But we do that all the time with our calendars.

We think that what it means to be a good Christian is to always say yes. Yet that's not how Jesus lived His life. He regularly let needs go unmet. He didn't say yes to every request. Even when the crowds were clamoring for Him, He would withdraw to be alone with His Father.

So be intentional with your calendar. Schedule in *first* the blocks you need for family time, recreation, rest, and time for yourself.

Develop Your "No" Muscle

Go ahead. Try it. Put your tongue against the roof of your mouth and make the N sound. Now let the O blow from your lips. See! I knew you could do it.

As Anne Lamott says, "No is a complete sentence."[5]

This point is very personal for me. I've had a long battle with people-pleasing and approval addiction. After a lot of soul searching, I am now more aware that my aversion to "no" comes from poor boundaries, not embracing my limits, unclear values, lack of courage, and insecurity. I suffer from what I affectionately refer to as "terminal niceness."

What I'm finally learning is that saying no isn't unkind or uncaring. What gives me the power to say no is keeping my eye on the higher yes. Every time we say no to one thing, we create space to put our time and energy toward something we value more highly—a higher yes.

Let me give you a good question to wrestle with: "What are the higher yeses in your life that will become the filter through which you make decisions?" Write them down and share them with those closest to you.

The only way to have the courage to say no is to turn your values into resolve. Drive a stake in the ground and determine that you will not be driven by the fickle opinions of others. Discover the higher yes. If you wait until you're in the moment, you'll cave in.

Choose Slow

Slow is a choice we make. We are not the victims of a fast-paced life. We are the perpetrators. So *slow down*. Let me give you some practical suggestions that your mind and body are going to revolt against. Let me warn you: these ideas are going to sound crazy. But they are the path to a more relaxed body and a healthier soul. Intentionally

- ▸ drive behind a slow car,
- ▸ look for the longest line at the supermarket,
- ▸ walk slower,
- ▸ take a longer route home from work,
- ▸ go slow when tucking in your kids or reading them a story,
- ▸ eat slower,
- ▸ sleep slower (longer),
- ▸ slow down your quiet time/prayer,
- ▸ put space in your workday (schedule brief breaks between meetings),
- ▸ slow down your holiday/vacation.

This week, take the challenge to slow life down by three seconds. Just three extra seconds can turn the mundane into a moment. Just three extra seconds can turn the ordinary into extraordinary. I guess what I'm asking you to do is *take a moment to create a moment*.

Take one . . . two . . . three seconds longer to

- ▸ savor the flavor instead of gulping down your meal,
- ▸ hug your kids when you tuck them in,

▶ reflect on the blessings of the day,

▶ kiss your spouse after coming home from work,

▶ notice a cloud formation,

▶ sit in silence with God,

▶ linger over a sunset,

▶ loiter after a rich conversation with a friend,

▶ start your day with gratitude for another new day,

▶ sit in the awe of a beautiful painting or song,

▶ encourage someone who crosses your path.

Slowing down isn't easy. But it is so worth it. And it is worth fighting for.

We're not just fighting for a less frantic pace of life, we're fighting for a better life! Declare a new day and a new way of living.

Start now! There's an old Chinese proverb that says, "The best day to plant an oak tree was twenty years ago. The second best day is today."

REFLECTION/DISCUSSION QUESTIONS

1. How do you respond to John Mark Comer's statement that hurry and love are incompatible? What do you think he means by that?

2. As you think about the pace of your life, where would you place yourself on the line below?

1————————————————————————————————————10

Unhealthy Pace   Healthy Pace

3. What would a healthy pace of life look like for you? In what ways have you seen an unhealthy pace of life take a toll on you personally?

4. I gave you three practical challenges in this chapter.

   ▸ Grab your calendar by the throat.
   ▸ Develop your "no" muscle.
   ▸ Choose slow.

   Which one of these three do you need to work on? Why?

CHAPTER 12

Simplicity Isn't So Simple

The ability to simplify means to eliminate the unnecessary so that the necessary can speak.

HANS HOFMANN

I LONG FOR SIMPLICITY. But the combination of increased complexity and the increased speed of life makes simplicity seem elusive.

Everywhere I travel and speak to leaders and teams, I hear the same words over and over again. *Crazy busy. Exhausted. Overwhelmed. Overcommitted. No margin.*

And what I think we have all accepted is that our culture is not returning to a quiet, slower, *simpler* time. Complexity and speed are here to stay.

Here is the question I want us to grapple with in this chapter: In a world that keeps getting faster and more complex, how do I pursue *simple*? The older I get, the more convinced I am that the quality of my one and only life has a lot to do with this topic of simplicity. The stakes are way higher and the issue is way deeper than organizing your closet or decluttering your garage.

All my life I have been a type A, driven, ambitious, overachieving person. It's in my DNA. So I regularly overcommit and then end up resenting my self-inflicted reality. I am a fairly typical firstborn. The internal script I learned from my family of origin has contributed to my drivenness, which has in turn contributed to complexity in my life.

My drivenness has been both exhilarating and exhausting.

I have had countless moments of longing for a simpler existence, but it has often felt elusive. Honestly, simplicity hasn't felt very simple. But my heart and soul are drawn to a simpler life. My soul resonates with the picture that Thomas Kelly paints when he talks about a life of simplicity: "For over the margins of life comes a whisper, a faint call, a premonition of richer living which we know we are passing by. . . . We have seen and known some people who seem to have found this deep Center of living, where the fretful calls of life are integrated, where No as well as Yes, can be said with confidence."[1]

Before we go any further, I think it's important to clarify something. Simple does not equal easy. Simple is not synonymous with problem free or pain free. Even a cursory reading of the Gospels makes it very clear that life as an apprentice of Jesus is not an easy, comfortable journey. Following Jesus is marked by sacrifice, self-denial, spiritual warfare, and trouble. There is no Easy button when it comes to being a disciple of Jesus.

So, if simple doesn't equal easy, then what is simplicity? I'm so glad you asked! My favorite definition comes from my friend Mindy Caliguire. She writes, "Simplicity means taking action to align one's exterior world with one's interior values and commitment to God."[2] Let that sink in for a moment. What eliminates complexity and duplicity is getting to the place where my external decisions and behaviors are in sync with my internal values and priorities.

When my values get clear, decisions get simple. Not easy, but simple. Simplicity is not necessarily about doing less. It's about letting my true values and priorities become a filter for decisions, options, and actions.

Many discussions about simplicity begin with steps to declutter your external world. And while that may be helpful and make you feel better, it doesn't really get to the core issues of simplicity.

Simplicity is a dual journey . . . interior and exterior. Outward attempts at simplicity without inward simplicity (or clarity) will end up feeling hard and frustrating and usually end in failure.

One of the reasons that many people end up in confusion and complexity is that they don't really know who they are. For many of us, our identity ends up being defined by external voices that tell us who we should be. Those external voices that seek to shape us are myriad: coaches, parents, teachers, friends, social media, marketing ads, etc.

We all need external voices to help us get better. But there's a vast difference between an external voice that helps me get better and an external voice that takes root in my soul and begins to define my core identity and significance.

To avoid complexity and duplicity, I must first get clear about God's truth and purposes. In other words, I must get clear about what God expects of me and what He says about living a great life. I also must discover my wiring, calling, and the unique race that only I can run. It takes a tenacious commitment to both in order to move toward simplicity.

I want to share with you a little equation that has been extremely helpful in my pursuit of simplicity. These three words are simple to understand but extremely challenging to integrate.

CLARITY + COURAGE + CALENDAR = SIMPLICITY

Clarity

What matters to you? I mean, what *really* matters to you? What are things you really value? What are the "must dos" of your life? If I were to do a LifePlan for you, I'd spend some time defining your "must dos." I use two criteria for defining a "must do." First, these are the things that are clearly God's truth and purpose for you. For example, if you're married, a clear "must do" is to make your marriage a high priority. My marriage doesn't get the leftovers. I'm a champion and a cheerleader for my spouse and give some of my best energy to helping her experience all that God has for her. We don't do life shoulder to shoulder, as some kind of business partners who share responsibilities and happen to live in the same house. NO! We do life face-to-face and have an intimate, satisfying, and life-giving relationship. If having a great marriage truly is a "must do," then your decisions, actions, and behaviors must reflect that. Obviously, you won't do it perfectly, but you are crystal clear about a great marriage being a "must do," and that brings simplicity.

As the German-American artist Hans Hofmann eloquently said, "The ability to simplify means to eliminate the unnecessary so that the necessary may speak."[3] As in art, removing those things that really aren't a priority in life makes it possible to create space for the "necessary" to speak. I must trim the excess so there's room for the essential.

In his fascinating book *Chasing Daylight*, Eugene O'Kelly writes his memoir during the three and a half months between his diagnosis of brain cancer and his death.

> I wanted to mentor someone, even one person, with this knowledge I had gained. Knowledge about winding down relationships. About enjoying each moment so much that time seems actually to slow down. About the one thing that's more important than time (and I don't mean love). About clarity and simplicity.[4]

I hope you and I don't have to go through a terminal disease to discover the preeminence of clarity and simplicity.

Complexity is often the obstacle to us getting to clarity and simplicity. So to get to clarity, you must at least temporarily hold at bay the complexity and busyness. You need time to reflect, to think, to ponder, to process.

I fear that Robert Louis Stevenson was right when he said, "Most of us lead lives that two hours of reflection would lead us to disown."[5] There was a fascinating and somewhat humorous study done by the University of Virginia. Study participants were exposed to a mild shock, but one that was painful enough that participants clearly said they didn't like it and would even pay money to not experience it again. Then participants in the study were left in a room with nothing but the "shock button." No phone, no computer, no music, no television . . . *nothing*. Just them and their thoughts. Two-thirds of the men and one-fourth of the women chose to voluntarily shock themselves rather than sit in silence. *Unbelievable*. (Some of you will use this study to show conclusive proof that women are smarter than men.) Dr. Tim Wilson, who helped conduct the study, said, "The mind is so prone to want to engage with the world, it will take any opportunity to do so."[6]

During the time of the coronavirus, a tweet began to circulate from Dave Hollis that said, "In the rush to return to normal, let's use this time to consider what parts of normal are worth rushing back to."[7] It was a call to reflect, ponder, and process how we were living prior to the pandemic. It was a call to consider what truly matters and the kind of life we really long for. Maybe you could take the challenge to schedule a half day of personal retreat. Get alone. Get quiet. Spend time reflecting and writing down what truly matters to you. Get clear about the "must dos" of your life.

Courage

In our world of complexity and speed, the battle for simplicity never goes away. It will take an ongoing, relentless courage to pursue simplicity. It requires diligence and vigilance. The drift of your life is never toward simplicity; the drift is always toward complexity and clutter. Let me prove it to you with one word: *garage*. Just leave your garage alone for six months, and I guarantee you it will drift toward disorder and clutter. It becomes a giant version of a junk drawer.

It is possible to do the hard work of getting clear about what really matters to you but never actually implement it into your life. This is the difference between having a clear set of blueprints and actually beginning construction. What keeps a lot of us stuck isn't that we aren't clear about God's purposes or even what really matters to us. It's the inability to execute that keeps us paralyzed with complexity. Courage to execute fills the gap between plans and results, between wishful thinking and actual progress.

Here are some questions to help you think through changes you might need to make:

- Where are you overextended?
- What are you spending time and energy on that's not a core value or priority in your life?
- What are you doing simply because it's an expectation that others have put on you?
- What one thing, if you actually did it, would bring greater simplicity to your life?
- What do you sense you need to stop doing?
- What is it that keeps you from taking steps toward greater simplicity?
- Where do you sense there's complexity and clutter in your life?

This is your one and only life. Rise up! Take ownership of it. You can do this. Don't let small voices, people-pleasing, or going with the flow cause you to settle for a life you don't really want.

Calendar

At the end of the day, simplicity has to find its way into your schedule and calendar. Your calendar is where your time and your values converge. You need to stop looking at your calendar as simply a way to organize your time and commitments. It is a primary tool in helping you live out the life you long for. One of the most courageous steps you'll ever take is to gain ruthless control of your calendar.

One of the biggest regrets of my life is how often I let others control my calendar and time. Often, my schedule wasn't dictated by my values, calling, and priorities; it was controlled by the whims and random requests of others. My problem wasn't that I lacked clarity around what was most important to me. Most often, it was a lack of courage to execute on what was most important. I know you need to be flexible enough to respond to Holy Spirit moments when you're prompted to give time to an unplanned situation. That's not what I'm referring to. I'm talking about the times I said yes simply out of people-pleasing or approval addiction.

The thoughtful and purposeful arrangement of your calendar is a critical and strategic component of the pursuit of simplicity. I'm sure some will read this section and think to themselves, "My schedule is already out of control. Where do I begin in my attempt to move to simplicity?" I love the advice Paul Borthwick gives in his book *Simplify*: "Cut a firebreak."[8]

Firefighters get ahead of the fire's path and create a break so the fire will burn out.

I think what Borthwick is challenging us to do is get out ahead of our current commitments and begin to create a break where we can get our lives under control. Firefighters can't stop the fire where it is in this moment, but by getting ahead of the fire, they can stop it from having any new fuel. Maybe today, you need to look out a month or three months and create a firebreak. Stop saying yes to things that really don't align with your values and priorities. Are there some current commitments that could be canceled or at least postponed?

As I was finishing this chapter, I took a little time to just sit and reflect on my own journey with simplicity. I would say I've had at least fifteen years where the topic of simplicity has been an honest pursuit. There are still plenty of days, even now, when I feel like I blow it. But as I sit here in this moment, I love the fruit that has come into my life as a result of pursuing simplicity. I don't feel restless or frantic. I no longer live or die by what people think of me. I'm learning to say no and actually be okay with it. I think

I've actually stopped believing that "bigger and more" is always better. I'm clearer than ever about what *really* matters to me. I take time more regularly to ponder and reflect on how I'm living. And I've taken much more control of my time and calendar. Life just works better!

REFLECTION/DISCUSSION QUESTIONS

1. Mindy Caliguire said, "Simplicity means taking action to align one's exterior world with one's interior values and commitment to God." What is one interior value you hold that has implications for your exterior world?

2. I shared the simple formula that has been helpful in my life.

   CLARITY + COURAGE + CALENDAR = SIMPLICITY

   Which of those words do you most need to embrace to discover greater simplicity?

3. If you had to name the single biggest barrier to simplicity in your life, what would it be? Explain.

4. What is something unnecessary that you need to eliminate so that the necessary can speak in your life?

13

The Discipline of the Daily

The secret of your success is determined by your daily agenda.

JOHN MAXWELL

"EVERYONE WANTS A REVOLUTION. No one wants to do the dishes." Those words are etched on a sign in a New Monasticism community house. And they reflect the spirit of our age. There is a cultural obsession with wanting to be great. Everywhere you go, you hear words that tout the claim of being extraordinary. *Epic. Next Level. Life-Changing. Historic. Radical. World-Changing. Legendary. GOAT* (greatest of all time). And we are constantly being prodded to pursue greatness. Make a Difference. Leave Your Mark. Make Your Life Count. Go Big or Go Home. Ironically, these uncommon qualities have become part of our common lexicon.

The advent of social media has only added fuel to the fire in our quest to be extraordinary. Social media tempts us to airbrush our lives in order to create a larger-than-life persona.

It makes me think of the very sophisticated, classic movie *Elf*. A lot of things make me think of the movie *Elf*, but I digress. There's a scene where Buddy the Elf makes his way from the North Pole to New York City. He is wide-eyed and overwhelmed by all the sights and sounds. He happens by a rundown diner that has a neon sign in the window advertising the World's Best Cup of Coffee. With naïve exuberance, Buddy bursts through the door and announces, "You did it! You did it! World's Best Cup of Coffee. Congratulations." The truth is, at best it's an ordinary cup of coffee. Just because you slap the label "world's best" or "epic" or "legendary" on something doesn't necessarily make it so.

Don't misunderstand me. I don't think there's anything wrong with wanting to be the best at something. I desperately want my life to count. In fact, this entire book is dedicated to helping people not squander the one and only life that they've been granted.

Embrace Ordinary

My concern is that in our relentless pursuit to be extraordinary, we have minimized the power of the ordinary. In reaching for the stars to fulfill our destiny, we miss the discipline of the daily. Most of us won't have the opportunity to set a world record, or launch a foundation to dig wells in a third world country, or give millions in a philanthropic gesture. But all of us—every single one of us—can live a purposeful and meaningful life each day.

I think about a lady I know whom you have never heard of. Her husband makes a good salary, so she takes all the income from her part-time job and uses it to be generous toward others. I think about a friend of mine who cares for his father who has dementia. Eighteen years ago, he and his wife took his dad into their home, and they have been his caregivers. He recently told me, "We just want to make sure my dad is loved well." I think of another friend whose family delivered fruit, toilet paper, hand sanitizer, and masks to people during the coronavirus pandemic.

As Annie Dillard says, "How we spend our days is, of course, how we spend our lives."[1]

There was an ordinariness to Jesus's life that often gets over-looked. When Jesus invaded our planet, God placed Him in an ordinary family. His dad was a blue-collar worker. He was not born of human royalty and didn't live in a palace.

Jesus never ran toward the spotlight. He never did anything for the sake of being spectacular, although that was exactly what Satan tempted Him with when he enticed Him to jump from the pinnacle of the temple. Jesus never "set out" to be great. He *was* great. He never focused on drawing a large crowd or marketing His brand. He knew that unseen does not equal unimportant. He never preached a message of dream big, change the world. Go big or go home was not His vibe. His message was much more about choosing surrender than chasing spectacular. In fact, His primary message was die to yourself and follow Me.

Lately, I have been captivated by a couple verses in 1 Thessalonians:

> Make it your ambition to lead a quiet life: You should mind your own business and work with your hands, just as we told you, so that your daily life may win the respect of outsiders and so that you will not be dependent on anybody. (4:11–12 NIV)

How different from our cult of the extraordinary. It's interesting that Paul doesn't say make it your ambition to be epic. Or make it your ambition to be a world-changer. Nor does he inspire us to be ambitious about becoming mega-successful. No! Paul challenges us to be ambitious about living a quiet life. Not once in my life have I ever heard a conference speaker challenge me to go all out in leading a quiet life. But what if . . . what if we put our energy and focus and tenacity into a really good, quiet life every single day?

Notice the "so that" phrase in verse 12: "so that your daily life may win the respect of outsiders." What if the great contribution of our lives was a focused and purposeful "daily life"? What if the key to a great life wasn't an extraordinary moment that got tens of thousands of "likes" but thousands of ordinary moments that were "liked" by our heavenly Father?

I want to spend the rest of this chapter helping put some flesh on the phrase "make it your ambition to lead a quiet life." What does a "good life" look like on an unspectacular, ordinary Tuesday?

Ordinary is usually not a very inspiring word. But ordinary doesn't have to mean vanilla or bland or generic. And it doesn't have to be passive or apathetic or listless.

We need to reimagine the word *ordinary* and begin to see beauty and richness in the ordinary.

One of the things that makes the Christian life so hard is that it's so daily. Many of us win or lose the battle in the midst of the daily rhythms of our ordinary lives. And author Tish Harrison Warren once confessed, "What I need courage for is the ordinary, the daily every-dayness of life."[2]

Doing "Daily" Well

It just now dawned on me that the reason this is such a big deal to me is that I've been surrounded by people who have given me an up-close-and-personal view of being ambitious to lead a quiet life. For sixty years I've watched my parents model this, and for forty-plus years of marriage, I've watched my in-laws live out this verse. My parents, now in their eighties, still help clean their church, still lead a couple small groups (including one for young couples), and still practice gracious hospitality like few people I have ever known. My in-laws are every pastor's dream as far as church members. Even though they're in their late eighties, my father-in-law is part of a men's group. He and his sidekick "Suitcase" serve as part greeters and part hall monitors for the children's area on Sunday. And my mother-in-law still teaches a Sunday morning ladies' Bible study for more than fifty women. She spends more time preparing to teach those women than most pastors spend preparing their sermons.

There are two keys that make ordinary living extraordinary. The first is consistent faithfulness. Friedrich Nietzsche calls this a "long obedience in the same direction."[3]

Week after week, month after month, year after year. No fanfare and no hoopla and no spotlight. Faithful stewardship and internal satisfaction are their own reward.

The second key is to infuse ordinary, daily tasks with spiritual meaning. In other words, we carry out our ordinary lives and responsibilities as unto the Lord. Our everyday responsibilities and interactions are not random. They are opportunities to represent Jesus—to be salt and light. We bless, encourage, cook, pray, serve, work, clean, give, love, and care for others because it's how apprentices of Jesus live our ordinary lives. And when we're at our best, we do so with joy and gladness. Our good deeds are not random acts of kindness. They are infused with meaning because our ordinary lives matter to our extraordinary God. And that is enough.

In the Old Testament, there was a man who was by far the wealthiest of his generation. He had every experience and luxury that money could buy. As King Solomon writes the book of Ecclesiastes, he reflects on how much of life is meaningless and futile. In the fifth chapter, he says there is one thing he's found that is good:

> Even so, I have noticed one thing, at least, that is good. It is good for people to eat, drink, and enjoy their work under the sun during the short life God has given them, and to accept their lot in life. (v. 18)

Really, Solomon? What about chasing my dream and making a big splash and doing something epic? Eat. Drink. Enjoy my work. Not much inspiration or sizzle in those words. Solomon's words are pretty ordinary. Remember that this comes from a guy who has done it all, seen it all, and had it all.

Notice that at the end of verse 18, Solomon challenges us to accept our lot in life. There's something helpful in accepting that God in His goodness and sovereignty gave me the life I have.

I need a rhythm for the ordinary. I need discipline for the "daily."

So let's talk about a couple practical ways that we can do ordinary well.

Success in the Small Things

Commencement speeches are a dime a dozen. Typically, they're filled with meaningless platitudes and quite forgettable. But in 2014, Admiral McRaven delivered an unforgettable graduation talk. Last time I looked, it had over ten million views on YouTube. He shared some life lessons he had learned by being a Navy SEAL. His first point was, "If you wanna change the world, start off by making your bed." He went on to say, "The little things in life matter. If you can't do the little things right, you'll never be able to do the big things right."[4]

What small thing do you need to do better? What discipline could you integrate that would help you have a better "daily" life? Seriously. Name it and decide right now that you're going to start being more disciplined in that "small thing." Is it one of the following?

- ▸ Getting to bed on time? Getting up on time?
- ▸ Eating healthier in the evenings?
- ▸ Spending daily time with God?
- ▸ Unplugging from your smartphone at night?
- ▸ Exercising three or four times a week?
- ▸ Making your bed each day?
- ▸ Doing the dishes after each meal?
- ▸ Leaving the TV off one night a week?
- ▸ Having a weekly date night with your spouse?
- ▸ Proactively planning your calendar for next month?
- ▸ Calling your parents each week?

According to the authors of *Liturgy of the Ordinary*, "God is forming us into a new people. And the place of that formation is in the small moments of today."[5]

Micro-Habits

James Clear, author of *Atomic Habits*, says, "It is so easy to overestimate the importance of one defining moment and underestimate the value of making small improvements on a daily basis."[6]

The power of ordinary living is unleashed when we experience the "compound interest" of small changes. We often dismiss small changes because they don't seem to make a big change in the moment. If I eat a piece of chocolate cake today, it probably won't be noticeable on the scale tonight. But if I eat a piece of chocolate cake every day, the compound interest of my consistent, bad, small choices will definitely tip the scale.

We need a system in our daily lives that helps us become the people we long to become. If you want to get serious about developing good habits, I would highly recommend absorbing and implementing the teachings in *Atomic Habits* by James Clear. I believe it is the gold-standard book on habits.

Clear says, "Changes that seem small and unimportant at first will compound into remarkable results if you're willing to stick with them for years. We all deal with setbacks, but in the long run, the quality of our lives often depends on the quality of our habits."[7]

One of the quickest ways to start getting some traction in your daily habits is to practice something that Clear calls "habit stacking."[8] The concept is that you take something you already do every day and stack a new behavior on top of it. Since I travel a lot, I make a lot of trips to the airport. To the habit of that forty-five-minute drive, I'm adding the habit of checking in with people who matter to me. I usually make a couple calls to people on my way to the airport. Also, I have a pretty aggressive goal for reading books this year. So each morning I have my Kindle right by my chair where I do my quiet time. Once I've finished my time in Scripture, I try to read a couple chapters of a book. In addition, I've never been good at flossing, so I'm trying to stack flossing onto each time I brush my teeth.

By way of example, here are a few ideas that Clear offers:

- ► Exercise. When I see a set of stairs, I will take them instead of using the elevator.
- ► Finances. When I want to buy something over $100, I will wait twenty-four hours before purchasing.

▸ Minimalism. When I buy a new item, I will give something away. ("One in, one out.")[9]

The crucible in which a beautiful and rich life is formed is the discipline of ordinary habits.

So the next time you're tempted to dream about starting a revolution, just go do the dishes!

REFLECTION/DISCUSSION QUESTIONS

1. In 1 Thessalonians 4, the apostle Paul challenges us to make it our ambition to lead a quiet life. When you think about your world, what would a quiet life look like?

2. Paul also said that a quiet life would win the respect of outsiders. How can a quiet life win the respect of those who don't know Christ?

3. What small thing do you need to get better at? In your daily life, how could you practice habit stacking?

4. What is a daily task that you could infuse with greater spiritual meaning? How would you do that?

CHAPTER 14

The Divine Rhythm of Life

> You can't live life at warp speed
> without warping your soul.
>
> ANONYMOUS

YOU DON'T STAND A CHANCE. The gravitational pull is too strong. The winds of culture are blowing like a hurricane. Willpower and good intentions won't get the job done. I'm talking about our ability to resist compulsive busyness and obsession with speed. With the ubiquitous presence of technology, not only are our schedules on overload, but our minds are in overdrive. The entire "attention economy" of social media is built on the goal of making sure you never have one moment of silence or stillness. As Cal Newport says in *Digital Minimalism*, "The urge to check Twitter or refresh Reddit becomes a nervous twitch that shatters uninterrupted time into shards too small to support the presence of an intentional life."[1]

The honest truth is, the pace at which we're living is exhausting, and in moments of sober self-reflection, we secretly wish we could get off the treadmill of a frenetic way of living. I have great news for you. There is hope. You actually can experience a more life-giving rhythm. You can dial back the rpms of your life and live at a more enjoyable pace. Doesn't that sound good?

One in Seven

The great news is that God has given us a very practical strategy for slowing down and living from a more rested place. His strategy is a practice called the Sabbath. The speed of life and 24/7 accessibility make this ancient practice more relevant and essential to our lives today than to any generation in history.

But I have a growing conviction that I want to put on the table right from the beginning. Before we get into all the practical "hows" of observing the Sabbath, I want to throw down the gauntlet. I want to draw a line in the sand. If you don't develop a biblical and theological conviction about this teaching, I don't give you a chance of it becoming a meaningful part of your life. The seduction and enticement of filling every second are just too powerful. A survey from Microsoft found that 77 percent of young adults answered "'yes' when asked, 'When nothing is occupying my attention, the first thing I do is reach for my phone.'"[2] The only thing that surprises me about that statistic is that the percentage isn't even higher.

There is a certain irony here. The Sabbath was a gift from God to the human race. That God has to command the practice of observing the Sabbath is like someone commanding me to eat chocolate cake every week or mandating that I play golf every week. But there is something broken in us, especially in our generation. We don't know how to be still or relaxed or quiet. Rest seems illusive. We have a bent toward distraction, noise, accomplishment, and "doing," so much so that God actually has to command us to have a day that's more about "being" and resting.

I want to take a little time in this chapter to explore in Scripture this thing called Sabbath. I'm not sure if you grew up going to church or what your theological background is, but I grew up going to church—a lot. I listened to thousands of sermons and Bible studies. The Sabbath was a complete nonissue. I never heard one sermon or talk about it. I knew it was one of the Ten Commandments, but I just assumed it was one of those Old Testament things that we didn't do anymore. I lumped Sabbath into the same biblical category as the Old Testament's prohibition against eating shrimp. It was an ancient law for an ancient time.

For the first thirty years of my Christian life, the concept of Sabbath wasn't even a blip on my spiritual radar. I didn't personally know one person who practiced Sabbath. And my philosophy of life would have had no room for it. Life is short; there's much to achieve. I have to squeeze all I can out of every second of every minute. I'll rest when I get to heaven. When that's your mindset, there is no room for a theology of rest. All my life, I've been taught how to go and go faster; no one ever taught me how to stop. I had to hit the wall in order to start learning how to stop. Just like your car needs a gas pedal and a brake, so does your life.

So in recent years, as I've been on a journey to live from a healthy soul, I've spent a lot of time studying what the Bible says about Sabbath and rhythm. It's important for you to understand that God hardwired this concept of rhythm into all of creation.

A rhythm is a regularly repeated pattern. Your physical body is sustained by regular repeated patterns. You have a rhythm to your breathing—you inhale and exhale fifteen to sixteen times per minute. Your heart beats with a very predictable rhythm. When you get an EKG done, it measures whether your heart is beating a normal rhythm and strength. There's a regular repeated pattern of the ocean's tide going out and coming in. Much of the beauty of music is tied to rhythm. Farmers have an annual rhythm of planting and growing and harvesting.

In Leviticus 25, God commanded Israel to have a regular repeated rhythm even for the soil. Every seven years the physical dirt was to be given a Sabbath rest. Nothing was made to constantly produce. Everything God ever created needs rest and restoration. According to one writer, "Without exception, every animal species studied to date sleeps, or engages in something remarkably like it."[3] Here's the punch line: *you* were made to live in rhythm.

If your pattern is to disregard the divine pattern, you will pay a price. You, my friend, are not exempt. If you violate this principle, you will do violence to your body, emotions, relationships, and soul.

The biblical rhythm of the Sabbath is one in seven. One day in seven that is set aside to *not* work, to *not* worry about being productive, to *not* be in a hurry. It's one day every seven days that is set apart to rest, to focus on relationships, to unplug, to connect deeply with God, to delight in His good gifts, to slow down and relax.

Sabbath Anchored in Creation

To understand the Sabbath, we have to go all the way back to the beginning, to the account of creation. After God created the various elements of the universe, He declared that each was "good." When He created humankind, the crowning achievement of creation, He said it was "very good." But the first time God declares anything "holy," it is in reference to the seventh day when God stopped and rested. The first thing in the Bible ever called holy wasn't a person or a place but a period of sacred time that was set apart for rest:

> Then God blessed the seventh day and made it holy, because on it he rested from all the work of creating that he had done. (Gen. 2:3 NIV)

Obviously, God did not rest because He was exhausted and burned out from creating the universe. He was setting an example for us. He was modeling something that He wanted us to imitate. I like Mark Buchanan's take on why God rested on the seventh day. "Like a parent who coaxes a cranky toddler to lie down for an afternoon nap by lying down beside her, God woos us into rest by resting."[4]

A little later in the book of Exodus, we find God putting the Sabbath into His Top Ten List. It's the fourth of the Ten Commandments, and the one with the most explanation. It's one of only two commandments stated in the positive. It's the only spiritual habit mentioned in the Ten Commandments.

> Remember the Sabbath day by keeping it holy. Six days you shall labor and do all your work, but the seventh day is a sabbath to the LORD your God. On it you shall not do any work. (Exod. 20:8–10 NIV)

Notice that God puts value on work. We are hardwired to be fruitful and productive. In fact, I don't think you can really appreciate the Sabbath if you haven't worked hard the rest of the week. Part of God's design of Sabbath is that it would be a day to recharge our batteries and refill our tanks.

Then, in Exodus 20:11, God anchors the Sabbath in the creation rhythm:

> For in six days the LORD made the heavens and the earth, the sea, and all that is in them, but he rested on the seventh day. Therefore the LORD blessed the Sabbath day and made it holy. (NIV)

Notice the word *therefore*. That word is the connector between God's rest in the creation story and our practice of Sabbath. In other words, God is saying there's a rhythm hardwired into the universe that goes all the way back to creation. That rhythm is work, then rest. Produce, then replenish. Work hard, then unplug hard.

Sabbath Anchored in Relationship

In Deuteronomy 5, something quite interesting happens. Moses is listing again the Ten Commandments. It's pretty much identical to the list in Exodus 20, except for the commandment about the Sabbath. The commandment doesn't change, but this time

God doesn't anchor the Sabbath in the creation story. Rather, in verse 15, Moses says,

> Remember that you were slaves in Egypt and that the LORD your God brought you out of there with a mighty hand and an outstretched arm. Therefore the LORD your God has commanded you to observe the Sabbath day. (NIV)

So here's the question: What does being slaves in Egypt have to do with Sabbath keeping? There is actually a profound truth in verse 15. When the Israelites were under the ruthless bondage of the pharaoh, there was no day off, no downtime, no rest, no vacation, and certainly no Sabbath. They were slaves who worked all the time. They lived under the pressure of unreasonable quotas.

But now that they have been delivered and are under the rulership of the God of heaven, things are different. One of the things that God wanted Israel to understand is that He is not a slave driver. He's a benevolent Father who wants the best for His children. And one of the marks of God's goodness is that He commands His people to stop. God is saying, "My people rest." And there's a deeper message: their value to God is not just in what they produce. Their value is in their identity as the children of God. Even when they're doing nothing on a Sabbath, they are still just as valuable to God. *Rewind*. Read that last sentence again. Let that soak in.

For those of us who find our value in what we achieve, this is a game changer. It's a death blow to our performance mentality. I've been working hard to actually believe and rest in the fact that my significance to God is not based on how much I achieve or how hard I work. You see, when I'm observing the Sabbath, I am not Lance the Replenish guy. I am not Lance the life coach. I am not Pastor Lance. I am not Lance the provider. I am simply Lance . . . a child of God.

Jesus and Sabbath

A cursory reading of the Gospels might lead you to believe that Jesus rejected the Sabbath, because it seems like He was always getting into trouble for violating the Sabbath. But you have to remember that the Jews had developed dozens of arbitrary laws to define what it meant to "not work." Jesus refused to be bound by these human-made laws that missed the heart of the Sabbath.

Minister and lecturer Lynne M. Baab writes, "Jesus broke the man-made sabbath laws of His time most often for the purpose of showing mercy to someone in need."[5] And in all of the confrontations He had with religious leaders over the Sabbath, not one time did He ever reject or dispute the validity of Sabbath keeping. He never took the Ten Commandments and amended them to a list of nine.

The main thing Jesus taught about the Sabbath is in Mark 2:27: "Then He said to them, 'The Sabbath was made for man, not man for the Sabbath'" (NIV). Here is my loose paraphrase of Jesus's words: "I gave you the Sabbath as a gift, and now you guys have totally screwed this up and turned it into a religious burden." Sabbath is a "get to," not a "have to." It's meant to lighten our load, not be a load. It's about rest, not rules. I love how Kevin DeYoung says it: Sabbath is "an island of get-to in a sea of have-to."[6]

In Exodus, when the Israelites were wandering in the wilderness, God supernaturally provided food for them. He provided food in the form of something called manna. So that they wouldn't have to go out and work to gather manna on the Sabbath, God provided a two-day supply of manna on the sixth day of the week. Then we read,

> Some of the people went out anyway on the seventh day, but they found no food. The LORD asked Moses, "How long will these people refuse to obey my commands and instructions? They must realize that the Sabbath is the LORD's gift to you. That is why he gives you a two-day supply on the sixth day, so there will be enough for two days." (16:27–29)

I love the words of verse 29. "The Sabbath is the LORD's gift to you." And it is God's gift to *you*.

I hope that right now you'll put a spiritual stake in the ground. I hope that you're convinced that God from the beginning of creation established a rhythm that He hardwired into everything He made. And I hope you believe that He gave us a strategy in a practice called Sabbath. Decide that from this day forward you will fight for a lifestyle that includes the Sabbath. In the next chapter, I want to share some practical how-tos of observing Sabbath. But I want to close this chapter by leaving you with a quotation from Rabbi Abraham Heschel to ponder.

> Six days a week we wrestle with the world, wringing profit from the earth; on the Sabbath we especially care for the seed of eternity planted in the soul. The world has our hands, but our soul belongs to Someone Else.[7]

REFLECTION/DISCUSSION QUESTIONS

1. When you think about setting aside twenty-four hours every week for rest and replenishment, what thoughts and emotions does that stir in you?

2. What are three benefits you could experience from the practice of Sabbath?

3. Even when you're doing nothing on a Sabbath, you are just as loved by and valuable to God. What do you honestly think of that statement?

4. What is a next step you can take to make the practice of Sabbath a priority?

CHAPTER 15

The Best Day of the Week

> The Sabbath was made for man,
> not man for the Sabbath.
>
> JESUS (MARK 2:27 NIV)

ALWAYS DO WHAT YOUR FUTURE SELF will thank you for! Let that statement sink in for a moment. Make choices today, create habits today, take a step today that your future self will thank you for. In this chapter, I want to give you some practical help for integrating the practice of Sabbath into your life, and I promise that if you do this, your future self will rise up and call you "blessed." In the last chapter, I talked about the why and the what of Sabbath. Now I want to share about the how of Sabbath.

It takes practice to do Sabbath well. That might seem like a strange statement to make. Why would I need to practice stopping and resting? How hard can it be? It sounds so easy and simple to take a day and not work. It's not! In our day of hurry, busyness, smartphones, and 24/7 access to everything, it's hard to stop. For many of us, it's going to take a while to detox from our addiction to hurry and speed and noise and learn to actually love the Sabbath.

I remember back more than fifteen years ago when I started trying to observe a Sabbath. I hated it. I'm serious. I was so addicted to the adrenaline rush of a fast-paced life, it was excruciating to try to stop. Even if I cleared my schedule and made the decision not to "work," I didn't know how to clear my thoughts and heart. I had an internal restlessness that seemed out of control. When I began trying to practice Sabbath, I felt like a parked car whose engine was running while somebody was pushing the gas pedal to the floor and my internal rpms were redlining. What I'm trying to help you see is that it might take you some time to detox from your addiction to work, technology, productivity, hurry, and busyness.

But now, years later, the Sabbath feels different. When I have a week when I'm pushing hard and my days are full and my tank is feeling empty, I'll think to myself, *Sabbath is coming*. It is now the day of the week that I look forward to the most. In fact, as I write this chapter, my Sabbath is tomorrow, and I can't wait. I now look to the Sabbath with joyful anticipation. It's the day my soul gets replenished. It's the day my body gets rested. It's the day my energy gets recharged. It's the day my relationships get reenergized. It's the day my perspective gets recalibrated.

In Exodus 23 when God is commanding the Israelites to observe the Sabbath, He says, "It also allows your slaves and the foreigners living among you to be refreshed" (v. 12). I love that. When done well, Sabbath is a day to be refreshed and recharged and replenished.

In order to do Sabbath well and for it to be a life-giving experience, you need a game plan. The game plan I'm going to propose is not a set of rigid rules but rather a framework that I think anyone can use to architect a meaningful Sabbath experience.

Prepare

There is some work involved in getting ready to *not* work. When the writer of Hebrews is speaking of a Sabbath rest, he challenges us to "make every effort to enter that rest" (4:11 NIV). Anytime there's a special holiday like Thanksgiving or Christmas, we plan and prepare for it. Sabbath is like getting a holiday every single week. As Dan Allender says, "The best way to protect the Sabbath is to make well-anticipated plans."[1]

Maybe the most important preparation you can make is to get it on your calendar ahead of time. Because of my travel, I'm not able to observe the Sabbath the same day every week. It's critical that I schedule it so that I can practice the rhythm of one in seven. If you were to look at my calendar right now, you would find a weekly Sabbath on it for the next year. As part of putting it on my calendar, it's important that I call it the Sabbath and not a day off.

Interestingly, Isaiah 58 says that the Sabbath is not a day to just pursue our own interests. When you have a "day off" from work, feel free to do whatever *you* want. But a Sabbath day is different. God has already prescribed the elements of a replenishing and God-honoring Sabbath. A Sabbath is a sacred, holy day, not simply a free day. It's also fascinating to me that right after Isaiah says not to pursue our own interests, he says, "But enjoy the Sabbath" (v. 13). When we do Sabbath God's way, it is enjoyable, life-giving, and restoring.

When you're trying to establish a new habit, you need to create a system or structure that gives you the best chance to succeed. For example, if you're trying to eat healthy, you might need to go through your pantry and remove all the Oreos and Pringles.

Let me give you an example from the book of Nehemiah. After the wall has been rebuilt around the city of Jerusalem, Ezra brings out the book of God's law and begins to read it to the people. When they hear God's truth, they realize they have been living in disobedience and immediately repent. Then they take an oath committing to live by God's laws. And one of the commitments they make that day is to observe the Sabbath.

Fast-forward a few months. Nehemiah has been gone and now returns to Jerusalem. When he does, he finds that the people of Israel are completely violating the Sabbath. The Sabbath day doesn't look any different from the other days of the week. Work is carrying on and people are selling grain and peddling merchandise. Nehemiah harshly rebukes them for profaning the Sabbath. But Nehemiah doesn't just stop with a rebuke. He knows the temptation to work is strong, so he takes a very practical step to help them observe the Sabbath. He orders the city gates to be closed at the start of Sabbath on Friday night and not reopen until the end of Sabbath on Saturday evening. That way all the merchants can't come and go into the city when it is Sabbath. Nehemiah even goes a step further. He tells the Levites "to guard the gates in order to preserve the holiness of the Sabbath" (13:22).

So, what is your gate? What steps do you need to take to ensure that you and your family can observe a Sabbath? Maybe for you, the equivalent of shutting the gate is shutting off your computer or not checking your email. Or perhaps it's putting a firm boundary around the day on your calendar reserved for Sabbath.

What would it look like for you to prepare for Sabbath?

Stop

The Hebrew word *Shabbat* is not a deeply theological or hard-to-understand word. The Sabbath simply means to stop, cease, or quit. When you tell someone to "stop it," you are actually quoting Scripture.

For forty-plus years of marriage, my wife has told me that I don't know how to be still or relax. So to say that learning to stop has been a challenge is a massive understatement. I'm not quite sure why, but I've always felt this obsessive need to produce, get stuff done, accomplish, achieve, and "do."

Selah is a Hebrew word that many scholars believe is best translated as "pause." Sabbath is pushing the Pause button on my life. As Lynne M. Baab says, "Sabbath is God's gracious 'five o'clock whistle' that gives me permission to stop and lay down my tools, ready or not."[2]

In my experience, it's in learning to stop that I find the time and ability to reflect and think and listen and process the stuff of life. All week long the jar of my life is shaken and rattled and stirred.

But when I stop on Sabbath, it allows everything to settle, and life and priorities become clearer. Sabbath allows me to recalibrate and realign myself to God's presence and purposes. I love Mark Buchanan's insight on this. He says, "Reflection flourishes only in rest: stopping long enough to coax out and face things inmost and utmost, things hidden, things lost, things avoided."[3]

One day a week God invites you to *stop* doing the following:

- ► Producing more
- ► Striving more
- ► Making more
- ► Achieving more
- ► Chasing more

So give yourself permission to stop. God has!

Rest

The Hebrew word for rest, *menuha*, doesn't just refer to physical sleep or taking a nap. It also has in it the idea of tranquility. Sabbath isn't just about rest for my body, it's also about rest for my soul.

But let's spend a little time talking about physical rest. The truth is, a lot of us are sleep deprived. People in generations past slept much more than people in our day. Prior to the invention of the light bulb "the average person slept eleven hours a night. Yes: eleven."[4]

Think about this. God gives you permission to sleep in on Sabbath. After all, there's no exhausting to-do list waiting for you as you enter Sabbath. One of my favorite things on a Sabbath is a good, guilt-free afternoon nap.

It's intriguing that the Jewish Sabbath begins in the evening. From a Jewish perspective, rest is not the completion of an exhausting day as we drop into bed dead tired. Rather, a Jewish Sabbath pretty much begins with sleep and rest.

Mark Buchanan reminds us that rest "is also a relinquishment. It is self-abandonment: of control, of power, of consciousness, of identity. We direct nothing in our sleep. We master nothing."[5]

Stopping and resting is a poignant reminder that I am not indispensable. The world can get along fine without me for twenty-four hours.

Let's assume you live to be eighty. Fifty-two Sabbath days per year would be 4,160 days total. That is 11.3 years of restful days that you would have enjoyed. So maybe the most spiritual thing you could do right now is go take a nap.

Delight

What is life-giving to you? I love to ask that question when I'm coaching people or speaking to teams. Seriously, what fills your tank? What is it that, when you do it, you can feel your soul fill with delight?

I don't believe that a great Sabbath is lying on the couch all day binge-watching Netflix. I don't believe Sabbath is synonymous with inactivity. I do believe that on a Sabbath we slow down, we rest, we put our work aside, and we engage in different activities.

We do the following:

- Read different kinds of books
- Take a hike and enjoy the beauty of creation
- Listen to music that fills our souls
- Enjoy the fragrance of a Sabbath candle
- Take our time to cook a special meal
- Go for a long bike ride
- Saunter as we take a slow walk to nowhere
- Are present in an unhurried conversation
- Linger in our time with God
- Enjoy just hanging out with our kids or grandkids

Most Christians I know are delight deficient; they're not entertainment deficient, but they lack true delight that fills their souls.

Have you ever thought about the fact that God didn't give you five senses just for functional reasons? He didn't give you eyes just so you could see where you're going. He didn't give you a mouth just so you could take in food to keep your body alive. NO! God also gave you your five senses for delight reasons. He gave you eyes so you could experience awe and ears so you could hear that which is beautiful and taste buds so you could delight in good food and touch so you could experience affection and connection. Part of practicing Sabbath is putting down "duty" and turning to "delight."

I like Mark Buchanan's golden rule for Sabbath: "Cease from that which is necessary. Embrace that which gives life. And then do whatever you want."[6]

Worship

When I first started practicing Sabbath, if I'm honest, I mostly saw it as something to help me be healthier and not burn out. But I think there is another aspect of Sabbath that doesn't get enough airtime.

The best illustration I can give is the relationship I have with my wife. Because I travel a lot, much of our communication is through text messages, brief phone calls, or chatting by FaceTime. All of those are beneficial in helping us stay connected when we're apart. But none of those are close to the connection we feel when we get unhurried, quality time together.

I believe that Sabbath was given as a gift to us not only to make sure we can rest and replenish but also so that we would have quality time with God. When God hands down the Ten Commandments, He says that the Sabbath is a day dedicated to the Lord.

Then, in Exodus 31:13, the Lord says, "Tell the people of Israel: 'Be careful to keep my Sabbath day, for the Sabbath is a sign of the covenant between me and you from generation to generation. It is given so you may know that I am the LORD, who makes you holy.'"

The Sabbath is given so that we know the Lord more deeply. It's a day with less noise and less clutter and less obligation. We distance ourselves from the world and work, and as a result we can see and hear God more clearly. A little more quiet allows a little more space for God to meet with us. When, on a Sabbath, we stop striving and pushing and accomplishing, we put ourselves in a better position to receive from God. On Sabbath we turn from our work and we turn to worship.

Sabbath has deepened my walk with God. I am pretty disciplined to spend time with God on a daily basis. But on Sabbath, I tend to do the following:

- ► Listen more
- ► Linger over God's Word
- ► Take time to express gratitude
- ► Absorb the words of a great worship song
- ► Think more about the trajectory of my life
- ► Practice silence
- ► Meditate on a Bible passage
- ► Reflect on the past week
- ► Confess my sin
- ► Enjoy God more

If you're like me, you long for more of the kinds of things we've talked about in this chapter. The first step is to make a decision. A small change in direction, over time, can lead to a whole new destination.

But it's not enough to make a decision. You must develop a game plan and begin to practice. As James Clear says in *Atomic Habits*, "You do not rise to the level of your goals. You fall to the level of your systems."[7]

REFLECTION/DISCUSSION QUESTIONS

1. What are your biggest barriers to consistently practicing Sabbath?

2. What could you do on the Sabbath that brings you delight and is life-giving to you?

3. Of the five components I mentioned (prepare, stop, rest, delight, worship), which one most draws you to Sabbath? Which one is most challenging for you? Explain.

4. What would an ideal Sabbath look like for you? How would Sabbath look different from a day off?

Part 4

ENJOYING LIFE
with GOD

16

The Art of Hanging Out

> You must arrange your days so that you are experiencing deep contentment, joy, and confidence in your everyday life with God.

DALLAS WILLARD

I HAVE A CONFESSION to make. I have a ministry called Replenish that focuses on the soul care of leaders. When you're known as the "soul care guy," people make some assumptions about you. And at least in my case, many of those assumptions are false. People think you have this deep, reflective, contemplative life. They also assume that you're relaxed, laid-back, unhurried, and that you spend hours every day in solitude and prayer.

The truth is, in many ways I am the least likely candidate to be the "soul care guy." I have a driven, active personality. I've often worn my busyness as a kind of badge of honor. I am easily distracted and sometimes feel like I'm addicted to technology.

I've lived with "hurry sickness" most of my life, and my workaholism has caused problems in my marriage. I struggle to have a consistent prayer life. Drivenness, distraction, and doing have too often characterized me. I don't know that I have ever had a really deep thought in my life, and trying to learn the art of paying attention to my soul seems like a daily battle.

So in this chapter, I want to share with you a discipline that has been challenging for me, but one that I think I am finally getting better at. And most importantly, I see it bearing good fruit in my life. I get to have lots of conversations with Christians, and when I ask about their spiritual life, I get a lot of typical, surface answers. But when I begin to probe a little deeper, and people get honest, they often confess that their spiritual life is stuck, stale, and stagnant. It's not unusual for them to admit that they're just going through the motions and there isn't a meaningful connection with God. So if that's where you find yourself today, you are not alone. In this chapter, I want to share an approach to walking with God that has been helpful in getting my spiritual life "unstuck."

It all revolves around a discipline I like to call "The Art of Hanging Out." In the last chapter, we talked about the command of God to take a break from work. In this chapter, I want to help us consider what it looks like to pursue God in the midst of our busy everyday lives.

Your Highest Calling

The Art of Hanging Out is the deliberate choice to relentlessly pursue knowing and loving God as your first and highest priority. Jesus was crystal clear about this. He said the greatest command in all of Scripture is to love God with everything that is in you. So your highest calling is not to make a big impact with your life or to use your gifts to be a blessing to others or to raise a great family or to be generous with your money. Those are noble and worthy desires. But your highest calling, your top priority, is to have a loving relationship with God. To say it another way, you are first called to do life "with" God, not just life "for" God. What

I'm talking about transcends simply going to church or doing a daily devotion.

I love how Ruth Haley Barton describes spiritual transformation: "It is the process by which Christ is formed in us for the glory of God, for the abundance of our lives, and for the sake of others."[1] It is first "in us," and then as it creates *abundance* in our lives, God's work in us will be a blessing to others.

Therefore, you must learn the skill of tending to your soul and your soul's loving relationship with God. Your soul was made by God. Your soul was made for relationship with God. Your soul longs to know and be known by God. Your soul was made to be in connection with God.

A. W. Tozer, in his classic book *The Pursuit of God*, writes, "Come near to the holy men and women of the past and you will soon feel the heat of their desire after God."[2]

You can feel the heat that Tozer describes in the words of the apostle Paul in Philippians 3:7–8:

> But whatever were gains to me I now consider loss for the sake of Christ. What is more, I consider everything a loss because of the surpassing worth of knowing Christ Jesus my Lord, for whose sake I have lost all things. I consider them garbage, that I may gain Christ. (NIV)

You can feel the heat in King David's words in Psalm 27:4:

> One thing I ask from the LORD,
>   this only do I seek:
> that I may dwell in the house of the LORD
>   all the days of my life,
> to gaze on the beauty of the LORD
>   and to seek him in his temple. (NIV)

I don't know about you, but I really do want there to be that kind of spiritual heat and passion in my life. The spiritual heat Tozer talks about isn't just living the Christian life "for" God but actually doing life "with" God.

Let me use a marriage analogy that I think will help. I could do marriage "for" Connie by doing the things I think will please her. Things like making coffee for her in the morning, remembering her birthday, grilling her a good steak, mowing the yard, making sure to put the toilet seat down.

But I think we would all agree that doing good and noble tasks doesn't equate to an intimate, loving relationship. They could be *evidence* of a great relationship, but in many marriages, they've *become* the relationship. There is simply no substitute for quality time together. My marriage gets stronger when we practice the art and discipline of hanging out.

The Bible is filled with invitations for us to simply "hang out." All of the biblical feasts and celebrations are calls to "hang out" and soak in the presence and goodness of God.

The challenge in Scripture to remember or think or meditate or ponder is an invitation to hang out with God. In the examples below, I've added italics to draw this to your attention.

- "Study this Book of Instruction continually. *Meditate* on it day and night so you will be sure to obey everything written in it" (Josh. 1:8).
- "*Remember* the wonders he has done, his miracles, and the judgments he pronounced" (Ps. 105:5 NIV).
- "I lie awake *thinking* of you, *meditating* on you through the night" (Ps. 63:6).
- "I *remember* the days of old. I *ponder* all your great works and *think* about what you have done" (Ps. 143:5).

The goal of remembering and pondering and meditating is not to think hard about something but rather to have your affections raised and crank up the spiritual heat.

So what does this look like practically? After all these years of trying to follow and love Jesus, I would say there are two fundamental choices that have helped me most in pursuing a deep and affectionate love for Him.

Create Space for God

The first choice is the commitment to create undistracted and unhurried space in my life to "be" with God. Space is about time. Being unhurried is about a relaxed mindset. It's about learning the skill of "being present." I can't tell you how many times I have carved out time to be with God but found myself distracted, restless, and preoccupied. The truth is, I still struggle, but I am growing in my ability to be fully present with Him.

In the words of Dallas Willard, "Hurry is the great enemy of spiritual life in our day. You must ruthlessly eliminate hurry from your life."[3] Early in my ministry, I would've been puzzled by Willard's statement. Hurry is the sign of a person on the move. People in a hurry are people on a mission. Hurry is the symbol of progress. Hurry is reflective of kingdom urgency. After all, time is short. How can we *not* be in a hurry?

But now, after a half century of following Jesus, I understand why Willard singled out the issue of hurry. Hurry and busyness have usually been a subversive diversion in my life. They're intoxicating and often applauded by others. They've kept the adrenaline flowing and propped up my sense of importance while robbing me of the intimacy with God that my soul longs for.

Perhaps the definitive passage in the Bible about spiritually hanging out is Luke 10:38–42. It is the story of two sisters named Mary and Martha.

> As Jesus and his disciples were on their way, he came to a village where a woman named Martha opened her home to him. She had a sister called Mary, who sat at the Lord's feet listening to what he said. But Martha was distracted by all the preparations that had to be made. She came to him and asked, "Lord, don't you care that my sister has left me to do the work by myself? Tell her to help me!"
>
> "Martha, Martha," the Lord answered, "you are worried and upset about many things, but few things are needed—or indeed only one. Mary has chosen what is better, and it will not be taken away from her." (NIV)

I love Jesus's words: "Mary has chosen what is better." Mary had learned the value of hanging out. I am a modern-day Martha with a deep longing to be more like Mary.

Creating unhurried space doesn't always mean blocking large chunks of time in my schedule. It's more about being present and relaxed in moments dedicated to being with God.

It does mean taking control of our calendars and prioritizing times with God. But on a practical, daily level, three simple things have made a positive difference for me in connecting with God.

- ▸ Start with a couple minutes of silence. This is about quieting your spirit and your mind so that you're in a posture of being open to God. If you're new to this practice, you will find it more difficult than you might imagine.
- ▸ Put your phone and/or other electronic devices out of arm's reach. The invitation to hang out with God gets derailed and disrespected when I interrupt hang time with screen time.
- ▸ Take time to listen. A good soul question I've learned to ask in recent years is "How is God coming to me right now?" That question slows me down and opens my spirit. In a good "hang time," it's a dialogue, not just a monologue.

Engage Scripture Relationally

The second fundamental choice that has been helpful has been learning to engage Scripture relationally.

I grew up in a very Word-centered environment. We believed (and I still believe) that the Bible is authoritative, inspired, and infallible. We respected and revered the Word of God.

As a result, most of my life I have approached Scripture informationally, pragmatically, or obligationally.

- ▸ *Informationally*. The Bible was something to be studied. The point was to grow in knowledge and insight, which certainly has been valuable in my life.

> ► *Pragmatically.* We engage Scripture for some practical principles to make our lives work better. Usually, these are the verses that are highlighted or underlined in our Bibles.

> ► *Obligationally.* Reading the Bible becomes an "ought to." It's about checking the "quiet time" box. There isn't much heart; it is simply about duty.

In recent years, I've focused on a different way to approach Scripture. I try to come to the Bible more relationally and affectionately. I regularly remind myself that when I open the Bible I'm not just reading an ancient book, I am meeting with the living God *and* my heavenly Father.

When Connie and I first met, we were both in college but lived six hundred miles apart. And when we first started dating, there were no cell phones, no email, no Facebook, and no text messages. Being poor college students, we made a commitment to see each other once a month and do a thirty-minute phone call every week. There was no such thing as unlimited minutes, and the half hour was all we could afford. We did one other thing to ensure that we would stay relationally connected: we wrote a letter to each other every single day. That's right. Every. Single. Day. We still have shoeboxes full of those letters.

Each afternoon when I would go to the mailbox in my dorm, I knew there was a love letter waiting for me. And when I opened that letter, I can promise you I read it relationally. I knew that behind those words on a page was a person who loved me and had something to say to me. I never did a word study or parsed the words in her letter. I just read them relationally and my affection increased.

It has been a joy to learn to read the Bible more relationally and to linger over Scripture. As Jonathan Edwards puts it, "There must be light and heat."[4]

Our reading of Scripture should result in both revelation (light) and affection (heat). Engaging Scripture is not just about adding more information and truth to our brains. It is also about getting to know a person.

I want you right now to think of the most beautiful sight you have ever seen. Where were you? Can you picture it? Can you see it in your mind's eye?

For me, what comes to mind is a flight I was on several years ago. I was sitting next to the window and the pilot came over the intercom and said, "For those of you on the left side of the plane, if you will look out your window, you will see a spectacular sight. It isn't normally this clear, so you are getting a rare treat today." I happened to be sitting on the left side of the plane, and as I opened the window shade, I saw a breathtaking view of the Swiss Alps. I remember just sitting there taking in the beauty and soaking in the moment.

In those moments, I saw the Alps clearly. My sight was unobstructed, but something was going on inside me that was beyond truth and accuracy and information. I was moved emotionally and drawn to what I was seeing. I had to pause and just sit in awe.

Hanging out allows us to see God not just clearly but beautifully.

REFLECTION/DISCUSSION QUESTIONS

1. What three words would you use to describe your current relationship/connection to Jesus?

2. How would you say you're doing these days at enjoying life *with* God, not just doing life *for* God?

3. What gets in the way of your having "unhurried space" to be with God?

4. What is one thing you could do to make your hang time with God richer and more meaningful?

CHAPTER 17

Practice Makes Progress

It is so easy to overestimate the importance of one defining moment and underestimate the value of making small improvements on a daily basis.

JAMES CLEAR

HOW LONG DOES IT TAKE to become a Christian? A moment and a lifetime. There is a moment we often refer to as *conversion* when you are born again. In that moment, the Bible says that you move from spiritual death to spiritual life. Another passage says that I was transferred from the kingdom of darkness into the kingdom of light. It is not a stretch to say that is the most important moment of your life. It changes not only everything in this life but also your eternal destiny.

But you will spend your entire lifetime learning how to live as a Christian. It's a process that theologians call *sanctification*, which refers to the lifelong journey of becoming like Jesus. A popular quotation is "A Christian is never in a state of completion, but always in the process of becoming."

On August 12, 1978, I stood on the platform of a church in front of family and friends and said those life-changing words: "I do." And in that moment, I was married. At the ripe age of nineteen, I didn't have a clue all that I was signing up for, but it changed everything. You could say I was transferred from the kingdom of singleness into the kingdom of marriedness. But I have spent more than forty years learning how to be married and how to have a life-giving relationship with Connie.

In the last chapter, we talked about creating the right environment for spiritual growth: creating unhurried space and reading Scripture relationally. In this chapter, I want to talk about the importance of systematic spiritual practices (habits) that help us know Jesus, love Jesus, and become like Jesus.

It Isn't Always Warm and Fuzzy

If you've been a Christ follower for more than a week, you know that staying connected to Jesus is more challenging than it sounds. I think there are a lot of reasons that we can end up disconnected from Jesus. In my own life, these have been things like complacency, busyness, workaholism, lack of discipline, distraction, sin, my smartphone, lack of desire, passivity, and television. And that's just the list from last week.

We know all the good reasons we should spend time with God, but the honest truth is that it just falls off our radar. We get busy with all the other demands of life and our time with God gets pushed to the fringes, at best getting the scraps and leftovers. And then when we do try to spend time with God, we're distracted, preoccupied, restless, and even bored. And honestly, it can feel dry and mechanical.

Recently, I read in Exodus 24 the story of Moses going up on Mount Sinai to meet with God. When he gets up on the mountain, it isn't until the seventh day that God finally speaks. Six entire days Moses sits there waiting in silence. Six. Whole. Days. I get antsy after six minutes.

"Leaning in" to your marriage and pursuing your spouse can present some enormous challenges, but the reward of a rich and life-giving marriage is worth pushing through the challenges. "Leaning in" to your relationship with God will also produce wonderful results.

In your fast-paced, demanding life, building a life-giving relationship with God is not for the faint of heart. Spiritual practices are not simply what committed Christians do. NO! The goal is a rich and flourishing relationship with God.

Garden Tools Required

Spiritual habits like prayer, Bible reading, fasting, solitude, silence, meditation, and Sabbath are the means to doing life with God.

Minister and author Marjorie J. Thompson says, "Spiritual disciplines are like garden tools."[1] They prepare the soil and remove the impediments so that the soil of our souls is in a place where God can cultivate and grow us into the likeness of Jesus. In other words, we don't measure our spirituality by how many times this week we had our quiet time. Rather, the measuring stick is the slow, incremental progress toward Christlikeness.

Paul says it like this in 1 Timothy: "Train yourself to be godly. For physical training is of some value, but godliness has value for all things, holding promise for both the present life and the life to come" (4:7–8 NIV).

It is important to notice that Paul uses the word *train*. Training is not an end in itself. The goal is not to train. The goal is to get healthy or get in better shape. The goal of the Christian life isn't to become an expert in spiritual practices or become knowledgeable about the Bible. The goal is to love Jesus and become like Jesus. For training to produce any results, I have to show up and put in some effort. And for training to have any value, there has to be consistency. When you start training at the gym, nothing much seems to happen the first day or even the first week. However, consistency over time produces a major transformation.

There are a variety of spiritual practices that can be very helpful in developing a deep connection with Jesus. At the end of this chapter, I've provided a list of resources that will go into much greater depth on some of those practices and how you can implement them. I want to challenge you to pick up one of these resources and go into training.

The big question I want to try to address is the "how" question. I really do believe that in most of us there is a desire (even a longing) to have a deeper connection with our heavenly Father. But for a variety of reasons, our walk with God has ended up stuck and stalled. So after a half century of following Jesus, I want to share some practical thoughts that have been helpful in my life. Even after all these years, just like with my marriage, it isn't easy to stay connected. But these practical principles have been valuable in my pursuit of a deeper relationship with Jesus.

Habit and Heart

There are two tracks on which spiritual transformation runs. Sustained spiritual growth requires both *habit* and *heart*. It takes consistent spiritual practices and genuine heart desire for true spiritual connection to take place. Spiritual practices (habits) without heart lead to hypocrisy and legalism. Think Pharisees. Heart without habit leads to inconsistent growth and dependence on shallow emotionalism. It is in the convergence of heart and habit that true spiritual transformation takes place.

Here is a warning for longtime Christ followers. I have found that the older I get, the easier it is to get sloppy with my spiritual practices. Our years of walking with Christ can result in a kind of comfortable familiarity that leads to passivity. But we all need fresh connection to keep the relationship vibrant and meaningful.

Author Gary Thomas writes, "Salvation is free, but maturity comes at a price."[2] I wish I could tell you there was a pill you could swallow that would help you magically have an amazing connection to Jesus and drop twenty pounds. I would be dishonest if I didn't tell you that deep spiritual connection involves discipline and intentionality. You won't mature accidentally. You won't drift into Christlikeness. In the same way that you need a game plan for your health, your business, your retirement portfolio, or remodeling your kitchen, you need a plan for becoming like Jesus. This will mean arranging your days so that spending time with God becomes a priority.

For some of us, the word *discipline* has all the charm of a colonoscopy. But rather than seeing discipline as drudgery and burden, what if we saw it as the means to a beautiful and rich life?

I would also encourage you to think *integration*, not compartmentalization. In my early years, I saw my time with God as something I needed to do to start my day, kind of like brushing my teeth. But then once I checked the box of having my quiet time, I moved on with my day. In recent years, I've made a very strategic shift. I try to view my whole day as doing life with God. I want to have meaningful time throughout my day when I connect with God. That shows up in a variety of ways: silence, reflection, meditation, gratitude, prayer, reading Scripture, worship, confession, etc.

It's also been my experience that discipline can gradually increase desire. So often, we start from the place of our feelings and desires. If we feel like it, we do it. If I don't have the desire, I blow it off. But what I have noticed is that often in life it is our love (or desire) that follows the development of a habit, not the other way around.

A couple years ago, I was working with a church in Vail, Colorado. I know some of you are judging me right now, but yes, I was willing to make the sacrificial journey to do ministry in Vail. But I digress. Anyway, I was on a tight deadline trying to finish my book *High-Impact Teams*. So when I was done with my meetings at the church, I decided to spend a quiet evening getting some writing accomplished. This was also a season when I was really working hard to eat right. Once I was back at my hotel room, I pulled out the room service menu, and in the spirit of making good eating choices, I ordered baked chicken and broccoli. In about thirty minutes, my dinner showed up. When I took the cover off the plate, there was a beautiful piece of chicken and some steamed broccoli sitting there. And I thought to myself, *That looks delicious*. At that exact moment I had sort of an out-of-body experience as I thought, *Who are you? There isn't a french fry anywhere in sight.*

And you are thinking that broccoli and baked chicken look deli-cious. I don't even know you right now. You see, the discipline of eating healthy had actually transformed my desires so that now baked chicken and broccoli looked good to me. Here's the point. Discipline was the fuel for desire, not the other way around.

So let's talk about this idea of developing life-giving spiritual habits. In *Atomic Habits*, James Clear explains that "the quality of our lives often depends on the quality of our habits."[3] I think it would also be true to say that the quality and depth of your walk with God depends on the quality of your spiritual habits.

I can't begin to tell you how many times as a young Christian I would hear a sermon and get inspired to have a deeper walk with Christ. And I would make some ambitious goal, like reading through the book of Leviticus every day. Then, in three days, once the inspiration had worn off, so did my discipline.

For us to see sustained spiritual growth, we need a doable system. Clear explains, "The holy grail of habit change is not a single 1 percent improvement, but a thousand of them."[4]

If you are struggling in your walk with Jesus, let me encourage you to develop a system of small steps that you can consistently implement day after day. When establishing a new habit, Clear suggests starting with something that can be done in two minutes and that can be done *every day*. Perhaps it's starting with reading one chapter every day, or praying for just those in your immediate family every day, or starting your morning with two minutes of silence every day.

As we talked about previously, another strategy that Clear advocates is what he refers to as "habit stacking."[5]

Find something you already do every day and now begin to stack a spiritual habit on top of the current habit. For example, while brushing your teeth, you could express gratitude to God for five things every day. While you drive to work, instead of listening to talk radio, you could engage a worship song that draws you to God every day.

Start small, but be consistent. Have a system. Build these practices into your everyday routine. Don't become legalistic about this. If you miss a day, just get back at it the next day. But for most of us, the danger isn't that we'll become overly legalistic about spiritual habits. Our danger is that we'll get busy and blow off our spiritual practices. Here's a huge lesson I have learned in life: when you're trying to establish a new habit, structure (a system) is your friend.

I'm not sure where you are in your walk with God, but I hope this chapter can be a catalyst for you to go to school on spiritual practices. Pick up one of the resources I've recommended.

I want to close this chapter with a story from my friend Mindy Caliguire. She was in a small group of women, and one night their study was looking at a set of verses that compared life to a spiritual race. There were a couple accomplished runners in the group that night. So Mindy asked, "When you get to that point where you so badly want to give up, what do you do? How do you make it through the wall?" One of the women in the group quickly responded: "I know exactly what those moments are and exactly what I need to do to make it through. . . . You just take the next step. And then the next step. And the next step."[6]

You don't think about the finish line or how far you have to go or how the other runners are doing. You just take the next step. Perhaps that's where you are today. When it comes to your spiritual race, you just need to take the next step. When it comes to becoming more like Jesus, what's the next small step you can take *every day*?

REFLECTION/DISCUSSION QUESTIONS

1. As you look back over your last couple years as a Christian, in what ways have you grown spiritually?

2. If you were talking to a brand-new Christ follower about how to stay connected to the vine (Jesus), what would you tell them?

3. What does "train yourself to be godly" look like practically in your life?

4. What is one small step you could take to implement a life-giving habit in your relationship with Jesus?

RESOURCE LIST

1. *Spiritual Disciplines for the Christian Life* by Donald Whitney
2. *Celebration of Discipline* by Richard Foster
3. *Spirit of the Disciplines* by Dallas Willard
4. *Sacred Rhythms* by Ruth Haley Barton
5. *The Life You've Always Wanted* by John Ortberg
6. *Seeking the Face of God* by Gary Thomas
7. *Thirsting for God* by Gary Thomas
8. *Spiritual Disciplines Handbook* by Adele Calhoun

18

The Rotting Tree Syndrome

Few things are more infectious than a godly lifestyle.

CHUCK SWINDOLL

JIM DOWNING, one of the founders of the Navigators ministry, was asked, "Why is it that so few men and women finish well?" His response was profound. He said, "They learn the possibility of being fruitful without being pure. . . . They begin to believe that purity doesn't matter. Eventually, they become like trees rotting inside that are eventually toppled by a storm."[1]

What a powerful and sobering image. We could replace the word *purity* with *holiness*. *Holiness* is a word we don't hear as much in the church today. But I want to remind us that the word *holiness* isn't "old school," it's "biblical."

Because we don't use the word *holy* much these days, and because it can conjure up all kinds of strange notions, it will be helpful to define the term. *Holy* means "to be totally separate and distinct. . . . In a class all by yourself."[2] It is something special. It's the opposite of common or ordinary.

Only once in Scripture is a characteristic of God mentioned three times in succession. He is holy, holy, holy (Isa. 6:3). And it's not only a characteristic of God, it's an expectation of us.

First Peter 1:15–16 says, "But just as he who called you is holy, so be holy in all you do; for it is written: 'Be holy, because I am holy'" (NIV). When defining a term, sometimes it's helpful to also talk about what it is *not*.

When I was a young believer, I thought holiness was defined exclusively by what you didn't do. You could be a mean-spirited jerk, but if you didn't smoke, drink, cuss, or gamble, you were holy.

So instead of holiness being about a characteristic that reflects the heart of God, it became a characteristic that reflected the harshness of God. Holiness became a kind of legalism that defined the Christian life by a list of dos and don'ts. And just mark it down: always following close behind legalism there will be a judgmental and self-righteous spirit.

But the misunderstanding and even abuse of the word doesn't mean we throw it out. We need to recapture it, accurately understand it, and live it.

Why is this so important for us to understand?

- ▸ Because it is God's best for us. A life of personal holiness is the pathway to a deeply joyful and satisfying life. A pursuit of holiness protects us from the things that would harm us and connects us to the things that bring us life.

- ▸ Because we're laying the foundation *now* upon which we will live the rest of our lives. In other words, a commitment to holiness has a ripple effect. Holy choices and decisions today pave the way for a better tomorrow.

- ▸ Because it equips us for life's defining moments. As nineteenth-century pastor and author Phillips Brooks so poignantly says, "Someday in years to come you'll be wrestling with the great temptation, or trembling under the great sorrow of life. But the real struggle is here, now, in these quiet weeks. Now it is being decided whether, in the day of your supreme sorrow or temptation, you shall miserably fail or gloriously conquer. Character cannot be made except by a steady, long-continued process."[3]

Relationship Is Fuel for Holiness

So, what would personal holiness look like in the life of a twenty-first-century follower of Jesus?

It all begins with the pursuit of relationship.

Psalm 15:1–2 says,

> LORD, who may dwell in your sacred tent?
>> Who may live on your holy mountain?
>
> The one whose walk is blameless,
>> who does what is righteous. (NIV)

Psalm 15 connects holiness and intimacy. The one who dwells in the sacred tent and constantly abides in God's presence is the one who is holy. A biblical discussion of holiness does not begin with rules, it begins with relationship. Many of us have tried to stay pure because of the fear of consequences. But that never has staying power. It has taken me a long, long time to learn this, but we are to pursue holiness out of love and relationship.

My desire for holiness is not driven by legalism but by love. The ultimate motivation of holiness is not the fear of consequences or getting caught. The motivation to pursue holiness is to protect the relationship I have with my loving Father.

My motivation for purity in my marriage is not just the consequences that would come if I were unfaithful to Connie. Rather, my desire to be holy in my marriage is driven by the reality that unfaithfulness would violate and put a huge wall in this intimate love relationship that the two of us enjoy. Holiness begins with us pursuing connection to and intimacy with God!

Holiness Is an Offensive and Defensive Game

Holiness requires us to play both offense and defense.

Psalm 15 says that the one who can constantly abide in God's presence is

> the one whose walk is blameless,
> who does what is righteous. (v. 2 NIV)

Playing defense means protecting myself from anything that could harm me, my relationship with God, and my testimony with others.

This means that you and I can't be naïve to the fact that we are vulnerable and exposed. I don't care how long you've been a Christian, you can't let your guard down. That's why Paul admonishes us to "work toward complete holiness because we fear God" (2 Cor. 7:1).

Many years ago, my wife and I watched an old suspense thriller, *There's a Stranger in the House*. It's about a killer who is targeting young college girls living in a sorority house. Police mount an all-out manhunt to find the murderer. Ultimately, they trace a phone call made by the killer from inside the sorority house! While they were combing the entire city, the murderer was living in the attic and wreaking havoc from within.

I must be aware that I still have an old sin nature that rears its ugly head and seeks to wreak havoc from within. The battle for holiness isn't just external, it is also internal.

But a pursuit of holiness isn't just about playing defense. You never win a game with defense only. The psalmist said in Psalm 15:1–2 that the person who can "live on [God's] holy mountain" is the person who "does what is righteous" (NIV). Personal holiness isn't just about dodging evil, it's also about doing good. Think about Jesus's life. What made His life holy wasn't only the lack of evil but His righteous acts of goodness.

We must have a practical game plan.

Solomon challenges us with these practical words:

> Guard your heart above all else,
> > for it determines the course of your life.
>
> Avoid all perverse talk;
> > stay away from corrupt speech.
>
> Look straight ahead,
> > and fix your eyes on what lies before you.
> Mark out a straight path for your feet;
> > stay on the safe path.
> Don't get sidetracked;
> > keep your feet from following evil. (Prov. 4:23–27)

That sounds like a game plan for personal holiness.

I once read an article about a battle fought by some Australian battalions during World War II on the southeastern coast of Borneo. After they had taken the enemy's territory, one of the most critical steps was securing the perimeter.

The article mentioned that the only means of securing this perimeter was by "constant offensive patrolling." I like that phrase *offensive patrolling*. You must offensively, proactively patrol the perimeter of your life. So what does that look like practically?

Holiness Down in the Trenches

- ▸ *Stay as far away from temptation and sin as possible.*
  When speaking about the seduction of a temptress, Solomon wisely advises us, "Keep to a path far from her, do not go near the door of her house" (Prov. 5:8 NIV).

  Don't knowingly put yourself in situations where you know you will be tempted to compromise your personal holiness. Establish some immovable guardrails in your life that will keep you out of the ditch.

- ▸ *Pre-decide how you'll handle temptation when it does show up.*
  You can't always control your circumstances, and moments of temptation will show up unannounced. There

are no ominous clouds, no tornado warning, no smoke alarms or voices from heaven.

That was true for King David. "One evening David got up from his bed and walked around on the roof of the palace. From the roof he saw a woman bathing" (2 Sam. 11:2 NIV). We aren't told the day of the week, or the season of the year, or the time of night. It's simply "one evening"; just an ordinary, run-of-the-mill, nothing-special evening.

That's usually when temptation happens. That's why you better know beforehand how you're going to handle it. You must pre-decide, because if you wait until you're in the heat of the moment, you will usually make a bad decision. Decide ahead of time that you are going to do what is right. Throughout my life, I've learned to ask a question that has served me well. When faced with a dilemma or temptation, I ask myself, "What's the right thing to do?" Most often, I clearly know the answer to that question. Then it is a matter of obedience. "Blessed are those who act justly, who always do what is right" (Ps. 106:3 NIV).

▸ *Be ruthless in guarding yourself against small compromises.*

A number of years ago, I was talking with a friend who had given in to an affair. He said, "I remember the exact instant we crossed the line that opened the door to a full-fledged affair." He then described a moment at the end of a meeting when he put his hand on hers, and he could tell she was receptive to his subtle flirtation. Of course, the truth is, he had crossed the line in his mind long before that moment when he took action. But that small compromise in that one moment led to devastating, life-altering consequences.

In Ephesians 4:27, when Paul is talking about anger, he says, "Do not give the devil a foothold" (NIV). A foothold is a small piece of ground. It is a little bit of territory that allows more territory to be taken.

I recently watched a documentary called *Free Solo*. It's the fascinating story of Alex Honnold, who free-climbed (without any rope) El Capitan in Yosemite. El Capitan is a mass of granite three thousand feet high. No one had ever done this before. He meticulously practiced and mapped out his route up the face of El Capitan, and as he practiced, he was always looking for a place where he could get a foothold. Sometimes it was no more than an eighth-of-an-inch piece of granite that was jutting out, but it was just enough to help Alex get a foothold.

Here's the big problem: *a foothold can become a stronghold*. The best strategy is to avoid footholds so that strongholds never need to be broken.

It's kind of like the *Titanic*. That historic disaster wasn't just a collision with an iceberg. There were three million faulty rivets that held the outer steel to the ship's hull. The steel company, in order to save a little money, used substandard iron. The rivets catastrophically failed. Life is all about the rivets. It's the small details and decisions that hold our lives together.

That means not cheating around the edges of your life. That means deciding against committing small indiscretions or telling little white lies or fudging on your expense report.

As someone who's followed Jesus for half a century and led in the church for over forty years, I have a concern. I fear we have overreacted to legalism. And now, in many places, the church culture is only embracing freedom and liberty. Our reaction against rules-based Christianity has made us sloppy when it comes to personal holiness. And in many places, in our desire to be relevant to the culture, we have become just like the culture. The heart of holiness is that we are to be different, set apart. I realize that there is a dance we must figure out when it comes to the Christian life. We must embrace our freedom in Christ but also be soberly aware that our freedom is not license to push the pursuit of holiness out the door.

▸ *When you blow it, own it.*

Another thing that troubles me about our culture is that we keep relabeling everything so we take out any personal responsibility. As long as I can label it a "disease," I can be the victim.

There is no holiness without contrition and repentance. Psalm 51 records the humble words of King David after he had committed adultery and arranged a murder. In Psalm 51, he owns his stuff. He says in verse 4, "Against you, you only, have I sinned and done what is evil in your sight" (NIV).

Repentance stares down the darkness of my own heart and my propensity to cut corners and act with less than full integrity. But repentance also clings to the hope and promise that God is full of grace and forgiveness.

With the one and only life you've been given, can I challenge you to renew your commitment to personal holiness? I know it's not easy, especially in the culture in which we're living. You will definitely find yourself swimming against the current of modern culture.

The writer of Hebrews called a group of Christians living in a complex culture to a holy life: "Work at living in peace with everyone, and work at living a holy life, for those who are not holy will not see the Lord" (12:14). Living a holy life is not for the faint of heart. It's hard work.

But it is the path to a great life and also the path of maximum spiritual impact.

Read the following verse slowly and out loud. It is a powerful verse about holiness. Every time there's a blank, insert your name.

"If you keep _____ pure, _____ will be a special utensil for honorable use. _____'s life will be clean,

and _____ will be ready for the
Master to use _____ for every good work"
(2 Tim. 2:21).

REFLECTION/DISCUSSION QUESTIONS

1. When you hear the word *holiness*, what comes to mind?

2. What is the difference between a pursuit of holiness rooted in fear and a pursuit of holiness rooted in
   relationship?

3. In this chapter, you were challenged to establish some immovable guardrails in your life that will keep you out of
   the ditch. What is an example of an immovable guardrail
   you need in your life?

4. You were also challenged to be ruthless in guarding yourself against small compromises. Where can you be tempted by a small compromise?

19

When Losing Can Mean Winning

Surrender is not the best way to live; it's the only way to live. Nothing else works.

RICK WARREN

THE YEAR WAS 1781. British General Lord Cornwallis led his weary and battered troops toward the Virginia coast. After a series of raids, the British troops occupied Yorktown. American and French troops led by General George Washington encircled them. They defeated the British troops and overtook Yorktown.

On October 19, General Cornwallis surrendered 7,087 officers and men, 900 seamen, 144 cannons, 15 galleys, a frigate, and 30 transport ships. Pleading illness, he did not attend the surrender ceremony. As the British and Hessian troops marched out to surrender, the British bands played the song "The World Turned Upside Down."[1]

Surrender. It's an ominous and intimidating word. It can conjure up images of raising white flags and laying down arms. It can make us think of giving in and giving up. Defeat and humiliation often go hand in hand with surrender. So, when we talk about surrender being a nonnegotiable of the Christian life, it can sound hard and harsh—unless we're surrendering to something better. The apostle Paul talks about surrender (total commitment) in Romans 12:1 when he says, "Therefore, I urge you, brothers and sisters, in view of God's mercy, to offer your bodies as a living sacrifice, holy and pleasing to God—this is your true and proper worship" (NIV). Offering your body as a living sacrifice is no small thing.

In ancient times, when animals were offered on the altar, the sacrifice was total and final. There was no such thing as partial surrender. That is the imagery in Romans 12:1. Paul is calling on us to willingly crawl up on the altar and offer ourselves in total and final surrender.

This call to offer our bodies as living sacrifices is bookended by two interesting phrases. First, he says that we offer ourselves "in view of God's mercy." Surrender is in response to God's mercy. When you really grasp what you were saved from, when you deep down feel the undeserved and free grace that liberated you from your sin, surrender is a response of gratitude. Surrender is saying to God, "Because of all You've done for me and in me, everything I am and everything I have I gladly surrender to You." Secondly, Paul says that our surrender is "true and proper worship." The words used here carry the idea that our surrender is logical or reasonable or acceptable. If God really is the King, Ruler, and CEO of the universe, and if He really did send His Son to die for me, then it is logical for me to surrender to Him as an act of worship. God wants the same place in my life that He already has in the universe. And that is reasonable.

Our problem is that we tend to focus on what we're giving up rather than what we're getting in exchange. What we fail to understand is that total commitment (surrender) is the way for us to experience God's best.

Epic Surrender

I want to take you to one of the epic moments of surrender in all of history. This moment happens in the book of Genesis to one of the patriarchs of our faith. His name is Abraham, and this experience left an indelible imprint on his life.

Through a promise from God, Abraham miraculously became a father at the age of one hundred. Even more miraculous is that his wife, Sarah, was ninety when she gave birth to their son, Isaac. And little Isaac became the apple of Abraham's eye.

All of us love our kids, but when you thought you would never have a child and God miraculously shows up and gives you a child, there's a kind of love and attachment that is deeper and stronger. Nothing delighted the heart of Abraham more than to watch this baby grow into a strong adolescent.

Then we read these three ominous words: "God tested Abraham" (Gen. 22:1 NIV). God drops an unexpected bomb into Abraham's life. Abraham is minding his own business, doting over his son, living the dream, when God shows up and disrupts everything. Abraham is about to have an encounter that he didn't ask for and certainly didn't want.

In Genesis 22:2, God says, "Take your son, your only son, whom you love—Isaac—and go to the region of Moriah" (NIV). It's like God goes out of His way to heighten the pain of this moment . . . "*your* son," "your *son*," "your *only son*," "whom *you love*."

Then God speaks the unspeakable: "Sacrifice him there as a burnt offering on a mountain I will show you."

Many of us are very familiar with this story. Don't let your familiarity somehow lessen the absolute horror of this moment. How could a loving God ask such a cruel thing? What if God were to ask you to kill one of your kids or grandkids? All of a sudden, this story gets *real*.

What isn't recorded for us is anything about that agonizing night after God told Abraham to sacrifice his son. As a dad and grandfather, I can only imagine how Abraham wrestled with

God and had it out with God. Nothing about this made any sense. Isaac was the one promised to carry forward the lineage of Abraham.

If you have walked with God very long, you know that He almost never reveals His entire plan to us. We're forced to wrestle with this fundamental question from God: "Will you trust Me?" Even when you can't make sense of what is happening.

To hear some preachers today, you would think that becoming a Christian is all rainbows and unicorns, and that health and wealth are God's will for everyone. And following Jesus is all about blessings and soaking up the good life.

I don't want to pop your bubble, but God's primary interest is not your comfort, it's your character. It's not your happiness, it's your holiness. It's not your prosperity, it's His purposes.

God's primary concern is for you to become like Jesus. And He will use struggle and pain and health problems and a lost job and a rebellious child and a challenging marriage and a jerk of a boss to build your character and make you more like His Son.

Let's go back to the story. Early the next morning, Abraham gets up and loads the supplies onto his donkey. They head off for Mount Moriah. It takes three days to get there, and I can only imagine the agony of every step. I suspect Abraham kept hoping that God would call off this ridiculous assignment. When they get to the place of sacrifice, Abraham, out of sheer obedience, builds an altar and prepares the wood. And then he ties up his son Isaac and lays him on top of the wood.

The test still isn't over. Heaven is silent. Abraham takes the knife and raises his arm, and from everything we know, Abraham is going to carry out this unthinkable act of killing his only son. But an angel of the Lord yells out, "Abraham! Abraham! . . . Do not lay a hand on the boy. . . . Now I know that you fear God, because you have not withheld from me your son, your *only* son" (vv. 11–12 NIV, emphasis added).

The Bible never says this specifically, but you sense that maybe Isaac had become an idol in Abraham's life. God doesn't mince any words when He rejects idols. In fact, this is such a big deal that it makes it into God's Top Ten List, known as the Ten Commandments.

At its core, idolatry is misplacing my affection, my devotion, my worship, and my love. It's putting something else on the throne of my life. As Martin Luther pointed out, "Whatever you set your heart on and put your trust in is truly your god."[2]

That's one reason God asks for total surrender. He knows it is not in our best interest to worship anything other than Him.

Surrender = Total Commitment

Whenever we look to something other than God to fulfill our deepest needs, satisfy our longings, give us hope, or define our identity, we have slipped into idolatry. "You must not bow down to them or worship them, for I, the LORD your God, am a jealous God who will not tolerate your affection for any other gods" (Exod. 20:5).

God is not jealous "of you," as though you had something He wanted or needed. He is jealous for the relationship. God wants an exclusive relationship with you. He is not okay with your devotion and worship being split.

Imagine for a moment that I put the picture of another attractive woman on my computer screensaver. And Connie walks by, and she sees the picture.

Let me tell you what her response will not be: *Well, that's odd, but Lance has a right to his privacy. His other relationships really aren't my business. Who am I to nag him about his personal life?*

NO! I promise you that would not be her response. With some passion and anger and righteous indignation, she would demand some answers. Inherent in our marriage commitment is an expectation of undivided devotion. When God sees us giving other things the devotion and worship He deserves, there is a righteous jealousy. It shows how precious our relationship to Him is.

In Genesis 22, Abraham demonstrated that he had undivided devotion to God. He passed the test.

For many of us, our moment of conversion and our moment of surrender don't happen at the same time. I became a Christian as a junior high kid. I had heard the gospel explained many times, and on that day I felt the tug of the Holy Spirit nudging me to say yes to Jesus. And I did. As much as I understood at that moment, I said yes to following Jesus.

But as my understanding of the Christian life grew, I began to understand that God wanted more for me than to just be saved and on my way to heaven. I began to grasp that God wanted me to surrender (or totally commit) all that I am and all that I have to Him. I can still remember the moment. I was sixteen and a junior in high school. I don't remember what day of the week it was, but I do remember it was early morning, before school. I was reading my Bible and knew God was calling me to surrender. I had full awareness that surrendering had huge implications for my career choices, how I spent my money, whom I would marry, and a host of other life decisions. In that moment, I surrendered *everything* in my life to His will and purposes. That moment was a huge game changer in my spiritual journey. The irony is that in surrender, I felt amazing freedom. I would do life God's way and under His authority. I have certainly fallen at times into rebellion and disobedience, but that day as a sixteen-year-old kid, the forever trajectory of my life was one of surrender to a good God.

The kind of surrender I'm promoting is a win. It's like the difference between a white flag and a wedding. Both are symbols of surrender. The white-flag surrender is one of defeat and giving up. It represents what you lose. A wedding is a different kind of surrender. In a wedding, you surrender your heart out of love and relationship. It is not at all about what you lose but rather what you gain. God wants you to know that His challenge to surrender is about a wedding, not a white flag.

Surrender Reframed

So, I want to reframe how you think of surrender.

God doesn't ask you to surrender so He can show you that He's in charge or as a sign of defeat. He asks you to surrender because He knows that is the path to the "abundant life" He offers.

The supreme example of surrender is not the story of Abraham and Isaac. It's the story of Jesus, who surrendered the glory of heaven and came to earth. He surrendered the privileges of deity and became a man. He surrendered His life for a cruel death on a cross.

Imagine Jesus watching this scene in Genesis 22, knowing that one day He would be the sacrificial lamb. And when His moment came, He would willingly surrender His life. But this time there would be no angel to stop the sacrifice.

There's just one final thing I want to point out. There is no such thing as partial surrender. Whenever Jesus called people to be His followers, He asked for total commitment and surrender.

He wasn't looking for fans, He was looking for followers. A fan is defined as an enthusiastic admirer. Jesus has a lot of fans. Fans don't surrender.

But when you read the Gospels, you quickly discover that Jesus was never really interested in having fans. He wanted followers. He cared about the commitment of the people who followed Him. When you become a follower of Jesus, your life is no longer your own.

Luke 9:23 says, "If anyone would come after me, let him deny himself and take up his cross daily and follow me" (ESV). That is follower talk, not fan talk.

Perhaps in an old Western movie you've seen a group gathered around a table in a smoke-filled saloon. They're playing poker. One of the guys takes a long, hard look at his cards, and then he does something radical and bold. He takes his entire stack of chips and pushes them all into the center of the table. He's betting everything he has.

This image demonstrates what it means to surrender your life to Christ. As Chip Ingram says, "The drama doesn't really get started and the action doesn't really begin until you say to God, 'I'm all in!' It's when you take the chips of your family, your future, your money, your gifts, your dreams, and all your possessions and you push them to the middle of the table."[3] You are saying to God, "I trust You and Your good plan for my life." And what you will discover is that surrender isn't a loss, it's a win.

REFLECTION/DISCUSSION QUESTIONS

1. How is surrender the path to the abundant life God offers?

2. God called Abraham to obedience and surrender even
   when he didn't have the whole picture. Describe a time
   when God led you to do something without your having
   the whole picture.

3. Share an experience where God used something difficult to
   produce something good.

4. Have you ever had a moment when you went "all in" and
   surrendered to the lordship of Jesus in your life? What was
   the fruit of that decision?

CHAPTER 20

Surviving Unhappy Endings

Grace grows best in winter.

SAMUEL RUTHERFORD

HER REAL NAME WAS VERONICA BOWERS, but her friends and family called her Roni. You have likely never heard of her. She served with her husband, Jim, as a missionary in Peru.

One of Roni's disappointments was that she was unable to have children of her own. But the couple was able to adopt a little boy they named Cory. Then the Lord doubled their blessing by allowing them to adopt a little girl they named Charity.

Just after Easter, Jim, Roni, and Charity flew to the border near Brazil to obtain a permanent visa for Charity. On the flight back home, the Peruvian military mistakenly believed that the plane was carrying drugs and took aggressive action. The fighter jets opened fire on the small Cessna, and more than fifty bullets penetrated the plane.

The plane began a downward spiral and crashed into the Amazon River. As the plane sank into the murky waters, Jim was able to pull Roni and little seven-month-old Charity from the plane. But he found a bullet had gone through the back of the plane into Roni's back and through her heart. That same bullet then pierced the skull of little Charity. They were both killed instantly.[1]

Here are an innocent seven-month-old baby and a thirty-five-year-old woman who had sacrificed so much to serve as a missionary in a difficult part of the world. If you allow yourself to linger very long over stories like this one, you find yourself asking some very hard and uncomfortable questions.

The reflex question is why. It seems so senseless. Where is the fairness and justice? In cynicism, some of us might have some challenging questions for God. "Here is a woman who dedicated her life to serving You and this is her reward? Where were You when this happened? If You could have prevented it, why didn't You?"

Stories like this one surface a lot of raw emotion and cause us to ponder some of life's most profound questions. These questions have been around a long time. But they're as current as today's news.

If you're going to live the life you deeply long to live, you must figure out how to prepare for and walk through times of suffering. The truth is, none of us knows when something might invade our life that puts us on our back (physically or metaphorically).

So if you're looking for the warm, fuzzy, Hallmark-card chapter, this isn't it. But what we are going to talk about is real-world stuff, and at some point in your faith journey, your world will be rocked and you will find yourself asking some of these hard questions.

I've followed Jesus for more than half a century, and there have been many situations I didn't understand. But one thing I understand full well is that being a Christian doesn't insulate you from life's problems. We, too, can be left with some deep and troubling questions. I think it's important that we be honest about that.

It is not helpful when we offer platitudes or simplistic answers to life's most complex questions. I want us to take a look at real Christianity down in the trenches of life. I don't want to airbrush our faith or show you only the pictures that are pleasant. That is not life. Life is not always clean, rational, or pleasant. Many biographies don't end with the words *they lived happily ever after.*

This is not a topic just for people facing the issues of cancer, death of a child, or a lost marriage. You could just be feeling stuck in a marriage that's going nowhere. You could be facing infertility. There could be a situation that has left you financially devastated. Perhaps you've had a long battle with depression. It could be any situation where life doesn't make sense and you can't see what God is doing. How do you cope when life doesn't work out like you had hoped and prayed?

There are two simple statements that I am convinced God would say to us when life doesn't work out like we thought it would.

"Let Me Be God"

We must begin with having an accurate understanding of God and His character.

Do you remember a few years ago when "glamour shots" were popular?

I was visiting in a pastor's home, and one of these "glamour shot" photos was on the fireplace mantel. Just as I started to ask who it was, I realized it was the pastor's wife. What they did to that photo wasn't just a glamour shot or makeover. It was a full-on magic trick.

Some of us are carrying around a glamour shot of God. Our view of God has been airbrushed and barely resembles the real thing. The view we carry in our heads reflects more how we want God to look than what He is really like.

It is important that we let God speak for Himself.

"Let Me Be God . . ."
"Because I Am in Control and Decide What I Allow into Your Life"

The Bible is absolutely clear that God is in control over the affairs of the world and over the details of your life. The situation, whether personal or global, has not caught God off guard or surprised Him. God is not up in heaven wringing His hands, wondering if this is going to all work out.

> You can make many plans,
>   but the LORD's purpose will prevail. (Prov. 19:21)

Have you ever noticed that God doesn't always consult you or follow your plans? There's nothing wrong with planning. In fact, the Bible talks about the value of planning. But we need to hold our plans loosely because God's purposes always trump our plans.

> All the people of the earth
>   are nothing compared to him.
> He does as he pleases
>   among the angels of heaven
>   and among the people of the earth.
> No one can stop him or say to him,
>   "What do you mean by doing these things?" (Dan. 4:35)

The Bible is crystal clear that God is the sovereign King of the universe and that nothing happens to me or to you without His allowing it.

Some people, because of their pain, have decided to give God a makeover. They can't reconcile the pain in the world with a God who is all powerful. Rabbi Harold Kushner gave God a makeover in his bestselling book *When Bad Things Happen to Good People.* After watching his son die of the disease progeria, Kushner concluded that "even God has a hard time keeping chaos in check," and that God is "a God of justice and not of power." Millions of readers found comfort in Kushner's portrayal of a God who seemed compassionate, albeit weak.[2]

Elie Wiesel, a holocaust survivor, said of the God described by Kushner, "If that's who God is, why doesn't he resign and let someone more competent take his place?"[3]

I don't know about you, but there isn't much comfort found in a God who is kind but powerless. Nor does such a view reflect the

God of the Bible. The very essence of what it means to be God is to have absolute power and control and sovereignty.

We don't get to vote or barter or negotiate on the matter. Suffering simply happens. We cannot choose when and how we will suffer or how long we may have to endure. But we can have confidence that God has a purpose for our suffering.

God is unapologetically in control and has a plan for history . . . and for *your life.*

"Let Me Be God . . ."

"Even Though I May Not Explain Myself"

You're likely familiar with a man in the Bible named Job. The Bible states that Job was the most righteous man on earth. One day Satan came before God and said, "The only reason Job serves You is because he's got it made. He's living the dream. Take all that away and he will curse you." So God allowed Job to be stripped of everything.

In one day, all of his livestock was stolen or destroyed. So in one disastrous moment, his wealth vanished. On the same day he learned that all of his servants had also been killed in a raid. While he was getting reports of these disasters, a messenger came in and delivered the devastating news that all ten of his children had been killed in a freak windstorm that collapsed the house they were in.

Then, as if that weren't enough, Job lost his health; the Bible says that he was covered with sores from head to toe. Now, it's important to note that Job was not privy to the conversation in heaven. In this moment, he had no understanding of why this was happening.

For the next thirty-five chapters, we have a front-row seat as Job wrestles with the age-old questions of pain and suffering. His friends say that his problems are a result of sin. Job goes through times of deep depression and grieving. There are times when he demands that God answer him. There are times when his faith surges and he declares his loyalty to God. There are moments when he loathes that he has ever been born. Chapter after chapter goes by, and there's no response from heaven. The silence is deafening.

Finally, in chapter 38, God speaks. What will He say to Job? I can think of several helpful things God could have said: "Job, I'm truly sorry about what's happened. You've endured unfair trials and accusations, and I'm proud of you." A few compliments, a dose of compassion, or at the least a brief explanation of the conversation that transpired "behind the curtain" —any of these would have given Job some solace and understanding. God says nothing of the kind.

God doesn't explain. He explodes. He doesn't answer one of Job's questions. God doesn't reveal His grand plan, He reveals Himself. He doesn't share His purpose, but He does reveal His power. For the next four chapters, He speaks of His greatness, character, and sovereignty.

God's message is basically this: *I'm God and you're not. And I don't owe you an explanation.* As hard as it is to accept, there are going to be some questions that we'll carry to our grave.

Sometimes when you're dealing with a person or family in crisis, you may feel like you need to explain what God is doing. You may feel like you have to make sense of what they're going through. I have learned that the most important things you offer to people in crisis are your presence and love. Let's just face it, sometimes there are no words or even Bible verses that can possibly explain or wipe away the pain people experience.

God says, "Let Me be God," but He also has something else He wants to say to us.

"Trust Me"

This is not an easy step. Sometimes the gap between personal pain and biblical promises becomes so wide that no bridge seems able to cross it. Nor is this a once-for-all step. Trust can at times be a moment-to-moment struggle.

In my opinion, the pinnacle moment in the book of Job happens in the thirteenth chapter. Nothing has changed in Job's circumstances, but his faith and trust surge, and he puts a spiritual stake in the ground.

Though he slay me, yet will I trust in him. (Job 13:15 KJV)

Job has a moment when he chooses to trust God when all of life screams that he should not. There is a humble willingness to leave some questions unanswered.

"Trust Me . . ."
"Because I Am Good"

At the heart of this chapter is a fundamental question: Is God good? Is He a caring, attentive, compassionate Father, or is He a distant, removed, sadistic, unfeeling, and impotent deity?

When Jonathan, my son, was little, he would stand on the window ledge in our kitchen and leap into my arms. He would fearlessly jump without hesitation. Why? Because he had jumped hundreds of times and I had never dropped him. He knew me and that I could be trusted. That game isn't as fun now that he's six three and in his thirties, but you get the point.

> The Lord is close to the brokenhearted;
> he rescues those whose spirits are crushed. (Ps. 34:18)

More important than finding God's purpose in your pain is finding God's presence in your pain. Some of us need to rest in the reality that God's face is toward us. He hasn't forgotten. He is present. He hasn't checked out. You can trust Him. He is *good*!

"Trust Me . . ."
"Because Heaven Is Real"

> For our present troubles are small and won't last very long. Yet they produce for us a glory that vastly outweighs them and will last forever! So we don't look at the troubles we can see now; rather, we fix our gaze on things that cannot be seen. For the things we see now will soon be gone, but the things we cannot see will last forever. (2 Cor. 4:17–18)

In generations past, one of the favorite topics for Christian songs was heaven. For so many Christians, down through the years, life had been incredibly hard, and what gave them hope was knowing that someday they would be with their Father in heaven.

But in our world, most of us have had comfortable and convenient lives. Without even realizing it, we begin to put our roots down deep in this world, and thoughts of heaven are far from us. It's often through pain that our world is rocked enough that we gain new perspective. We realize that we are mortal and that we won't be here forever. We come to see, as Scripture says, that life is like a vapor, here today and gone tomorrow.

When life gets hard and unbearable, the Lord's encouragement to us is to remember that we are not home yet.

Philip Yancey writes, "The Bible never belittles human disappointment . . . but it does add one key word: temporary. What we feel now, we will not always feel. Our disappointment is itself a sign, an aching, a hunger for something better. And faith is, in the end, a kind of homesickness—for a home we have never visited but have never once stopped longing for."[4]

I don't fully understand why, but God has determined to do some of His most significant work through pain and suffering. There are some things that God will do in you and through you only as a result of pain. Could it be that what the world really needs to see as much as a miracle or a healing is some people who find deep joy, peace, and trust in God in the middle of their suffering?

I want to take you back to Roni Bowers, the missionary tragically killed by a bullet from a Peruvian fighter jet. This is a paragraph from her journal written shortly before her death.

> Life doesn't always give you a storybook ending. You do not always end up with the answer to your prayers that you desire. God often chooses to do something different with your life than you envisioned. But it's ok. He's still God, and He still loves you. As long as your confidence in God remains strong in the midst of all the questions and myriad of emotions you will be ok. He is the only one who remains constant, and life is good if you stay in His arms— God's loving arms. You may not understand where He leads, but you will be safe and secure with Him anywhere, even in death.[5]

REFLECTION/DISCUSSION QUESTIONS

1. Since you started your journey of following Christ, how has your understanding of God changed? What led to that change?

2. When helping others through times of suffering, what are some things we can do that are helpful and what are some things we should avoid doing?

3. As Christians, we are not citizens of this world. Heaven is our true home. Practically speaking, what can you do to have a more eternal (heavenly) perspective?

4. As you reflect back over your life, what is something that was painful, bad, and maybe even evil that God in His sovereignty used for good?

Part 5

PRACTICING
the PRESENCE
of PEOPLE

CHAPTER 21

The Value
of Adding Value

To love another person is to see the face of God.

LES MISÉRABLES

WHAT A STRANGE BIBLE VERSE: "Without oxen a stable stays clean, but you need a strong ox for a large harvest" (Prov. 14:4). An empty stable is clean, but so what? A nice, sterile, sanitized stable misses the whole point of having a stable. Stables are built for livestock, and with livestock comes a mess. Do you see where I'm going with this?

God has given you a "stable," and it's your one and only life. You can keep it nice and neat and tidy. You can lock the gate and keep people out, but that's not how you were made to live. People are messy and complex, but they are so worth it. If you want success (a strong ox for a large harvest), the stable won't be nice and clean. Just like there's no real benefit to an empty stable, there's no benefit to a relationally empty life.

Years ago, there was a movie starring Jim Carrey called *The Truman Show*. Truman lived in an artificial world. He was in the dark as to what was truly happening. You see, his town was actually the set of a television show. The weather was perfect, the people were friendly, everyone was happy, and there were no problems in the fictitious town of Seahaven. Well, actually, there was one huge problem: his life wasn't real. It was sanitized and scripted and ended up leaving Truman feeling empty and longing for more. He intuitively knew there was something more that he wasn't experiencing.

Relationships with people plunge us into the real stuff of life—the messy, uncomfortable, frustrating, exhilarating, and rewarding stuff of life. Some of us have been hurt so badly that we have opted out. We've put up a wall and decided to keep a safe emotional distance from people. No doubt, engaging and loving people are fraught with peril. You will not escape this life unscathed and unwounded.

It is people and relationships that give life richness and texture. In fact, it's not a stretch to say our lives are defined by relationships. Generally speaking, life's most exhilarating, heart-pounding highs and most gut-wrenching, painful lows come from relationships. When you walk into somebody's home and look at the pictures on the wall or fireplace mantel, they are not photos of cars, jewelry, houses, or their local bank. They're photos of people. This is a poignant reminder that life's meaning is largely derived from the people we do it with.

The Invaluable One Adds Value

I love how Jesus modeled the importance of people and relationships in life. First, He stepped out of the glory and majesty of a problem-free heaven (clean stable) and invaded our planet and became like us. He became the God-man. Then His entire public ministry was spent up close and personal with messy, broken, needy human beings. The things that clearly mark the life of Jesus on our planet were His tenderness, patience, and unrelenting love for people. He truly valued people.

One of my favorite moments in the life of Jesus happens after His resurrection. It is the story of Peter and his conversation with

Jesus after Peter's gut-wrenching betrayal in denying Christ. Not knowing what else to do, Peter has gone back to a life of fishing. And Jesus comes after him. I love that!

My suspicion is that forever burned in Peter's mind was that moment when he denied Christ for the third time. The sense of failure was all-consuming. He was Peter, the rock; and now he was crushed and crumbled. He had taken pride in his courage, and when the moment of truth came, fear and panic ruled the day.

But now in John 21, after a night of fishing, Peter recognizes that it is Jesus standing on the shore. He impetuously dives into the water and frantically swims to Him. Out of breath and dripping wet, Peter is now standing face-to-face with the risen Jesus. But Peter is not all better. He failed miserably, and his denials are ringing in his ears. Perhaps he wonders if he can ever be used again. Will he ever recapture the special relationship he had with Jesus? He's not sure, but he knows he can't keep living like this.

Jesus had prepared breakfast, so they sit and eat. Finally, breakfast is over. No more small talk. Jesus turns and addresses Peter. Surely Jesus is going to talk about the elephant in the room (or in this case, on the beach). I suspect Peter's heart is racing, his stomach churning, and he has a lump in his throat. As far as we know, this is the first one-on-one conversation Jesus and Peter have shared since his denial.

It's interesting to me that Jesus never brings up Peter's failure. There's not one word of condemnation or "I told you so." I'm always struck by how tender Jesus was with people who were fragile.

We know that Jesus asks Peter three times, "Do you love Me?" and then three times He basically commands Peter to "feed My sheep." We could spend time dissecting the nuances of the various Greek words in this passage, but we might miss a simple but profound truth.

Think about this. Jesus knows He's about to ascend back into heaven. And the most precious thing to Jesus is people. They're created in His image, they're eternal, and they're the reason He left heaven. Now Jesus turns to Peter and says, "I want you to take care of these people who matter so much to Me." Despite Peter's ignoble failure, Jesus gives him a noble assignment. He places His most valued possession into the care of Peter. Jesus knows full well that He will be departing planet Earth very soon. Of all the possible jobs Jesus could have given to Peter, it's significant that the one assignment He gives him is to care for the messy, broken, confused sheep that Jesus loves so much.

Valuing People as Jesus Did

If we're going to truly live the life we long to live, we must see people as Jesus did and engage them as Jesus did. That means opening up our stable to the messiness and blessedness.

To really value people, we must add value to them. In other words, we must make their lives better. We must bring benefit. We must add meaning. I want to share with you three ways to demonstrate value and add value to people.

But before I jump into these three practical challenges, let me take a moment to talk about putting yourself in a place where you can add value. Your level of emotional health and self-care has huge implications for your ability to add value to others.

Emotional health is like having a good set of shock absorbers for your soul. When the shocks are working well, they help absorb life's bumps and potholes. But when your shocks are worn out and you hit a pothole, you bottom out and the ride is rough.

You also need to remember that when your soul isn't healthy, you make the ride rough for everybody else on the journey with you.

If you are empty and exhausted, you won't love people well. If you are insecure and insensitive, you won't add value to people, because you'll always be preoccupied with "you." When you enter into a conversation, it tends to be "here I am" instead of "there you are." When you are emotionally unhealthy, it never stays hidden. It always leaks out in irritation, defensiveness, impatience, and frustration. If you want to love people well and add value to people, you must pay attention to your own emotional health.

So let me share with you three practical challenges that will help you value and add value to people in your world.

Be Present

Over three hundred years ago, Brother Lawrence wrote his book on practicing the presence of God.[1] This simple book is about learning to be conscious of God's presence throughout your day. No matter how mundane or unspiritual the task, you can find God there. It's about staying present and lingering and not rushing past opportunities to connect with your Maker.

We need to learn the same practice with people. We need to learn how to stay present, to linger, to "be in the moment." This means being a good listener, physically stopping so that someone has our full attention, and not looking past them as they try to engage us.

I sometimes wonder how many people over the years have come to me because they had something on their heart and needed a caring prayer or a listening ear or an encouraging word. But I was scattered, preoccupied, and too busy to practice the presence of people. And though they would never say it out loud, they walked away disappointed and feeling like "he doesn't have time for me." We will never really see people if the room is filled with the smoke of distraction and preoccupation.

Attention is one of the most powerful forces in the world. There's a beautiful Old Testament verse that says, "The LORD bless you and keep you; the LORD make his face shine on you and be gracious to you; the LORD turn his face toward you and give you peace" (Num. 6:24–26 NIV). To turn your face toward someone is to give that person your complete, undivided, interested attention. It communicates value.

We are the only enemy when it comes to being present. We are not held hostage by some outside force or person. We have to stop being so preoccupied with the past and the future. We need to live more in the "now." Right here. Right now. This is where life is.

Slow Down

For those of us who are compulsive hurriers, slowing down is tough. I'm thinking about starting my own support group called Hurriers Anonymous. One good thing about the group is that our meetings would be short.

Do you walk fast everywhere you go? Do you multitask while talking on the phone? Do you often find yourself impatient when your schedule is interrupted? Are you obsessively always trying to shave a few seconds off any task? Even when you do stop to talk to people, do they sense that you're rushed, looking past them? If so, you could be a good candidate for our support group. Hurry is the archenemy of valuing people.

Here is a universal axiom: the faster you go, the less you notice.

When you're flying in an airplane at thirty-eight thousand feet and soaring at 500 mph, you can see a long way, but you lose the ability to see detail. You might be able to see a house, but it would look like a dot on the landscape. When you're traveling in a car at 65 mph, you can't see as far but you can see more detail. You can see that same house but now take in more specifics. You can see the color, the shape, possibly how many windows are on the front of the house, and if a car is in the driveway. But if you're walking down the street, you can actually stop and observe. You can notice a whole level of detail that isn't even possible from a moving car. You might notice the toys in the front yard, a dog in the yard, a rolled-up water hose, or the kind of flowers by the front porch. Who knows, you might even meet an actual person living in the house.

There will always be a direct correlation between the speed of your life and your ability to connect with the people God brings across your path. I'm always impressed with how Jesus connected with people. His days were not filled with thoughts of organizational goals. He never seemed frantic or frenetic. He just moved in the flow of the Spirit and always had time for people along the way. The pace of His life created space in His life . . . to be fully present.

So how about it? Can you dial it back a notch? Can you slow down the rpms? Can you put down your smartphone? Can you slow down enough to truly show value and add value to people?

Be Personal

As part of a church-wide campaign at Saddleback, we decided to take on the enormous task of feeding all the homeless in our county for a forty-day period. I remember going to a training hosted by our local missions team about how to work best with homeless people. They encouraged us not to just hand people a bag of food and supplies and then walk off feeling we could now check this off our list. We were challenged to stop and learn their name and then take the time to hear their story. The word they used in that training that stuck with me was *dignity*. When we actually stop and take time to engage someone's story, we help restore people's dignity. One of the definitions of *dignity* is "the condition of being worthy of respect, esteem, or honor."[2]

I soon realized that as important as the food was, just as important was offering respect, building esteem, and giving honor. By taking time to enter someone's story, we communicate to people "you matter," "you are important," "you are valuable."

Let me give you a challenge. Let's make it a thirty-day challenge. What if for the next month you really got serious about noticing people, paying attention to people, engaging people, truly connecting with people, hanging out with people, having rich conversations with people, and loving people?

Grab a friend and ask them to join you for this thirty-day experiment.

When I think about valuing people and adding value to people, I think of a man who had significant influence in my life as a young leader. He mentored a group of us college students. We met at his home on Tuesday nights around 9:30. We would talk Bible, life, and ministry. But Shelby also made it a point to occasionally get with us one-on-one. We would meet at a local diner late in the evening. On the occasions I met with Shelby, I don't remember any of the topics of our conversations, but I do remember something he did every single time. There were always college students there, studying and writing papers. As we would get ready to leave, Shelby would walk by some student's table and pick up their check and pay for their meal. It was a simple gesture that never cost more than a few bucks but showed value and added value to a poor college student.

Shelby modeled a great axiom of life: when we add value to the lives of others, we add value to our own lives.

REFLECTION/DISCUSSION QUESTIONS

1. How difficult is it for you to be vulnerable? Do you tend to keep people at a safe emotional distance?

2. Who has added value to your life? What did they do? Consider dropping them a note this week to express your gratitude.

3. How can your personal emotional health help or hurt when it comes to valuing people?

4. As you think about your personality and wiring, what can sometimes get in the way of you being present with people? What is one practical step you could take to be more present with people this week?

CHAPTER 22

You've Got a Friend

A friend is someone who understands your past, believes
in your future, and accepts you just the way you are.

UNKNOWN

FRIENDSHIP IS OVERRATED! That would be my conclusion
based on a sample group I've worked with over the last decade.
Several times a year, I facilitate a two-day process called a Life-
Plan. It's a holistic look at one's life and future. One of the life
domains we talk about is friendship. When the topic comes up,
the response is very predictable. The person sitting in front of me
usually gets quiet and sheepish. Often, what I hear in that moment are these words: "I know I should have some close friends,
but . . ." Then I begin to probe deeper and will ask, "Is it a felt
need or desire for you to have some close friendships?" My question is often met with a shrug of the shoulders and a passive
acceptance that close friendships sound nice but just don't feel
realistic. By the time people give energy to their jobs, spouses,
kids, chores, and church, there just isn't any energy left to pursue
a meaningful friendship.

Many of us had close friendships in our growing-up years and into our college (or early adult) years. But then life got busy, and for a lot of us, close friendship has been one of the casualties. That was certainly my story. As I pursued marriage and family and vocation, the number of acquaintances continued to build and grow like a good stock portfolio. But the number of deep, transparent, gut-level friendships began to fade like an old photo. In my relational world, I was wide but not deep.

You see, pastors like me typically don't go deep in friendships. We are rich in surface-level acquaintances but often bankrupt when it comes to authentic, life-giving, "you don't want or need something from me" friendships. Many have lives that are consumed with performing the duties of life and vocation, and they never get around to nurturing any deep friendships for themselves. For some, there's a fear of self-disclosure. Vulnerability feels risky, and it can be risky. Maybe you could give testimony about being betrayed by a so-called friend. So it's just easier to plow through life, head down, and embrace the illusion that "someday" you'll get around to developing a true friend or two.

One day, a somebody entered my life. And I actually enjoyed being around him, which seems fairly important when you're considering a friendship. I remember thinking, *I would like to spend time with Tim and get to know him better. I could see us being friends.* The decision to pursue that friendship was one of the best decisions of my life. It has now been more than a quarter of a century that we've done life together. For much of that time, we haven't lived in the same town. From the earliest days of our friendship, I have felt acceptance and connection. We bear the battle scars of true friendship. There has been growth, disappointment, challenge, laughter, and struggle. We've shared our hopes and dreams for our lives and for our kids . . . and now our grandkids. We've ruthlessly bantered with each other. We've developed a vault full of funny stories. We've celebrated victories together, and we have walked through painful disappointment together. It hasn't been all rainbows and unicorns. True friendship is hard, and there is a cost.

The Return on Investment of True Friendship

If you're standing on the outside looking in and doing a cost-benefit analysis of deep friendship, let me just tell you, it's worth the investment. And if you're on the inside, enjoying life-giving friendship . . . cherish it, nurture it, and celebrate it. It is a gift.

This whole conversation makes me think of a disabled man in Luke 5. We are not given his name. We don't know his parents. Not one word from him is recorded. We don't have any clue as to his personality or looks. His entire biblical biography is summed up in one word: *paralyzed.*

Every day, every single day, all day long he sits on his mat, which is probably about three feet by six feet. He is a prisoner inside his own body. Somebody else has to bring food to him. He can't dress himself. Anytime he goes anywhere he has to be carried.

Because he can't work, he depends on the compassion of others to throw a couple coins his way. He literally lives day-to-day. There's no hope of surgery or treatment or physical therapy or a breakthrough cure.

He has no job, no money, no influence, no status, and a pretty dim future. His life is going nowhere . . . literally. But he does have one thing going for him. He has people in his life who care for him and about him. He is part of a killer men's small group.

Ecclesiastes 4:9–10 provides us with an axiom about friendship:

Two people are better off than one, for they can help each other succeed. If one person falls, the other can reach out and help. But someone who falls alone is in real trouble.

You see, you will fall. You will stumble. You will end up on your back. You will get in a bind. You will find yourself in a crisis. That is not the time to look for a friend. That is the time you better have a friend. Jesus certainly modeled this for us. He tapped twelve men on the shoulder and invited them into relationship with Him— deep relationship. They did life together for three years.

Mark 3:14 says, "He appointed twelve that they might be with him and that he might send them out to preach" (NIV). The first invitation was for the disciples to be with Jesus, and out of that friendship, they would be sent to preach the Good News.

Here's what I know for sure about friendship. You will never drift into deep friendship. It requires initiative. Passivity is the enemy of deep friendship. If this is important to you, get after it. Be aggressive. Don't wait for someone to reach out. Be persistent and don't give up. Don't be a stalker, but be persistent. You need to own this for yourself.

Put Voice to Your Desire

You might need to articulate your desire to pursue a deeper friendship with someone. Now, if you're a guy, you might be thinking, *Are you kidding me? Why don't I just send one of my manly buddies an email with the question Will you be my friend? ___ YES ____ NO.* But before you write me off, I want you to hear about an ancient friendship between two manly men, Jonathan (the king's son) and David (the future king).

> And Jonathan made a solemn pact with David, because he loved him as he loved himself. Jonathan sealed the pact by taking off his robe and giving it to David, together with his tunic, sword, bow, and belt. (1 Sam. 18:3–4)

This would be like giving your friend your favorite sweatshirt, your tennis racket, and your shotgun. Notice that Jonathan made a "solemn pact." He didn't ask anything from David. This wasn't a utilitarian or transactional arrangement. It was a gesture of true friendship as he declared his commitment to pursue the friendship. We just don't do that today, but maybe we should.

A lot of good friendships have fallen by the wayside, not because of a big blowup but simply because we stopped pursuing and initiating. Maybe somebody's name comes to mind right now. You have a lot of time invested in that relationship and it has simply drifted. You didn't mean for it to happen, but it's now been months since you connected with that person. Maybe it's time to reinitiate the friendship. Give them a call today and set up a time to have lunch (and don't forget to take your favorite sweatshirt).

Get Real

I have a good friend who says, "For there to be true community you must be willing to open your kimono." I'm not sure that's the best word picture, but you get the idea.

If I'm going to live the life I really long to live, I'm going to need an intimate friend or two who fully knows me. I need a deep friendship with someone who isn't impressed with me and who isn't afraid to tell me the truth. I need a handful of people who know the junk about me, who know where I struggle, who know the skeletons in my closet, and who love and accept me anyway.

True friendship is going to require me to get real, to be vulnerable and honest. But we are all broken and have junk in our lives that isn't pretty, and we work very hard at making sure it never sees the light of day. Just like the guy in Luke 5, we all have a mat. We have those things that represent our brokenness. This man's weakness and brokenness were right out there for people to see. We spend a lot of time trying to hide our brokenness, trying to cover it up, trying to manage it.

It is risky to have someone carry our mat. They see our weakness and brokenness. So we keep people at a safe distance. We want to feel connected without the risk of vulnerability, of being exposed. Now, more than six decades into life, I have discovered that true friendship requires that we be known . . . fully known.

I personally struggle with this. It does not come easy for me to be open and transparent. I am calculated. Careful. Cautious. Always trying to carefully manage what you think of me. It took a long while before I fully opened my life to my good friend Tim. It was a long journey learning to believe that he could be trusted with the stuff in my life that was ugly. And it was a long journey to discover that he truly accepted me just like I was. Trust and acceptance have been the Velcro of our relationship and the ingredients that have produced life-giving vulnerability.

Let me ask you four questions that might help you assess how vulnerable you are.

- Who *really* knows you?
- Who knows where you're weak?
- Who knows where you struggle?
- Who knows where you're most tempted to sin?

Choose Inconvenience

Inconvenience is the price tag of deep friendship. Let me take you back to Luke 5 and our friend who's paralyzed. One day Jesus comes to town. There are lots of stories circulating about His teaching and His miracles. This guy's friends decide to go hear this intriguing rabbi. But then they decide they can't go without their paralyzed friend. Who knows? Maybe Jesus could do a miracle for their friend.

So they go get him. Each grabs a corner of his mat, and they head off to hear Jesus. They get to the house where Jesus is teaching, but the place is already packed. They can't see Him, and they can't hear Him.

I love what happens next. These buddies will not be stopped from getting their friend to Jesus. I imagine them huddling together to brainstorm what they can do to get their friend in front of Jesus. Friend #1: "We could tell them we're friends of the Messiah and have a backstage pass. No, that won't work. Backstage passes aren't a thing yet." Friend #2: "Let's find the handicapped seating section. No, that won't work. Seating for the disabled hasn't been invented yet." Friend #3: "Let's make a hole in the roof and lower him down right in front of Jesus." Paralyzed man: "Are you serious right now? Does anybody else have another idea? You want to carry me on my mat up on the roof? And then you want to dig a hole in the roof and lower me down from the ceiling? THIS IS A BAD IDEA!"

But that's exactly what they do. To everyone's shock, a mat with a body on it starts coming through the hole. Somehow they get him to Jesus without dropping him. Amazing!

You have to give these guys credit for creativity, for innovation, for ingenuity. And even more than that, you have to give them credit for pushing through inconvenience to create a life-changing moment for their friend. I don't know about you, but I want to have friends like these guys.

So, whom are you willing to go through the roof for?

Bring God into the Friendship

When this guy is lowered through the roof, Jesus obviously sees his broken body. But listen to the words of Jesus: "Friend, your sins are forgiven" (v. 20 NIV). This man has a need beyond the physical, and that is where Jesus goes first. The man has not only a broken body but also a broken soul. That is his greatest need. This man, who has probably felt helpless and worthless on many occasions, now has Jesus look him in the eye and say, "You are now right with God."

For Christ followers, deep friendship doesn't just lead to deep relationships with each other, it leads to a greater and deeper relationship with God as well.

We all need friends who bring us closer to Jesus. Are there some people you know who, when you are around them, make you want to love Christ more? They don't point you to themselves. They don't lure you away from God; they're actually like a spiritual magnet, drawing you toward God. They inspire you in your spiritual journey.

You might have a deep friendship or two, but you might need to take that friendship to a new level by bringing spiritual life and conversation into it. Talk about what God is doing in your life. Pray together. Share a passage of Scripture that has recently spoken to you.

Let me go back to that story in Luke 5 and make one other observation. After Jesus forgives this man of his sins, He says, "'So I will prove to you that the Son of Man has the authority on earth to forgive sins.' Then Jesus turned to the paralyzed man and said, 'Stand up, pick up your mat, and go home!'" (v. 24).

And *immediately*, he gets up. For the first time ever, his friends don't have to carry him.

It is Jesus and friendship that ultimately bring healing.

If these men had not brought this paralyzed man to Jesus, this miracle would not have taken place.

In your mind's eye, I want you to picture a moment. You're in your early seventies and the pace of your life has slowed. On this Tuesday, you get up early in the morning and sit at the kitchen table with a cup of coffee. The house is still and silent. No one is there but you and God and your thoughts. On this morning, instead of thinking about the day's activities ahead, you begin to reflect back on your seven decades of life. You worked hard. You tried to provide for your family. Life has certainly had some unexpected twists and turns. In many ways it has been a good life, but in other ways there have been hardships, disappointments, and regrets. One thought encourages you and brings a smile to your face. You are grateful to God that you took time to invest in a handful of deep friendships. And the ROI has been exponential. You realize that on the ledger of life, possessing cars and houses and clothes and stuff doesn't add up to much. But a real friendship is of high value. It's the stuff life is made of.

REFLECTION/DISCUSSION QUESTIONS

1. Who was your best friend growing up? What made that a great relationship?

2. How does the thought of being fully known by a friend sit with you?

3. How could you raise the spiritual temperature of a friendship that you currently have?

4. What is a step you are willing to take toward deeper friendship?

CHAPTER 23

The Power of a Word

Words create worlds.

UNKNOWN

VOICE IS A STRANGE and funny thing. In simplistic terms, there are two simple processes that create our voices. The larynx in concert with your vocal folds produces sound. Then, your tongue, teeth, velum, and lips modify the sound and out comes something we commonly call *words*.[1]

What I just described is the physical mechanics of voice, but it in no way begins to describe the impact of voice. Words create worlds. That age-old axiom poignantly and succinctly reveals the power of voice.

Every single one of us has felt the power of voice. Way beyond simply hearing and understanding words, words have found their way into our spirits and taken root there. We have personally experienced both the life-giving and the soul-crushing effects of words. Through the careless use of those sound waves, our words can tear down, viciously humiliate, create panic, spread mistrust, plant doubt, destroy a reputation, wound a heart, and spread hate. And yet, that same voice can inspire hope, demonstrate love, bolster confidence, express belief, communicate value, provide comfort, change perspective, and breathe life.

The words spoken to us in our past continue to echo in our present. For all of us, words spoken to us over the years continue to shape our lives today. We are way more fragile and impressionable than we want to admit. There's an old childhood expression that says, "Sticks and stones may break my bones, but words will never hurt me." That has certainly not been my experience or the experience of any person I have ever met. Solomon used only nine words to communicate the far-reaching influence of voice: "The tongue has the power of life and death" (Prov. 18:21 NIV). It is mind-boggling to think that air going across a vocal box and shaped by a tongue that weighs only 2.3 ounces could have such impact. Part of practicing the presence of people is to understand the weight of our words and then carefully use them.

Jesus's Final Benediction

It is not lost on me to notice the final words Jesus spoke while He was on our planet. This moment takes place just before Jesus is going to ascend back into heaven. He obviously knows that these are His final moments with His friends. If you had been on the Messiah advisory council, and you knew this was the last speech He would ever give, how would you have counseled Him to use His voice? What would you have suggested for this final talk? Perhaps Jesus should give them His three-year strategic plan for His global vision. There had regularly been infighting and jockeying for position among the disciples, so perhaps He ought to hand out an org chart so the disciples have clarity on lines of authority. Since the church would be launched soon at Pentecost, perhaps it would be wise for Jesus to pass out bylaws for how the church should function and be governed.

As important as each of those things might be, that is not what we find Jesus doing in these final moments on earth. Luke 24:51 says, "While he was blessing them, he left them and was taken up into heaven" (NIV). The very last words from the lips of Jesus on this planet were words of blessing.

Wow. What a contrast to the world in which we're living. The order of the day is vicious, mean-spirited vitriol. The erosion of civility and common courtesy has been rapid and far-reaching. Our smartphones and social media have only given a megaphone to the problem. We've made it easier than ever to verbally assault people while hiding behind a screen.

Words Speak Life

But the current cultural environment presents a tremendous opportunity for those of us who follow Jesus. We get to use our voices to speak words of blessing and hope and dignity and love. Every single day, you carry around with you two invisible buckets. In one bucket is gasoline and in the other is water. A wise person knows when to use each one. In a situation where there's anger, tension, and disharmony, we want to use the water of our words to put out fires of contention. But not all fires need to be extinguished. When it comes to believing in people, encouraging people, inspiring people, and valuing people, we want to pour gasoline on those conversations.

To really live the life you long to live, you need to help other people live the life they long to live. And one of the simplest and most effective means of doing that is through words of blessing. "Blessing" is all about the words we speak "to" and "over" the lives of people. Here's the great news. Anybody can be great at blessing. It doesn't require a certain level of skill or education. And it's not dependent on your title or position in the organization. You don't need a budget line item to succeed in this practice. The ROI on this is huge. For minimal investment, there's amazing return. Words of blessing have staying power.

As we have done so often in this book, I want us to take a look at how Jesus modeled this so well for us. Jesus is the guest speaker in the synagogue, and as He teaches, He notices a woman who the Bible says has been crippled for eighteen years and is unable to stand up straight (see Luke 13:10–16). Jesus calls her forward, lays hands on her, and she is instantly healed. You would expect in that moment for there to be spontaneous applause or shouts of praise. The very next words in the passage say that the synagogue leader is indignant because Jesus healed on the Sabbath. Are you kidding me? Everyone there just witnessed a miracle and this woman got her life back, and all this guy can say is, "You're not supposed to heal on the Sabbath."

Jesus defends what He did and has a sharp rebuke for this hypocritical spiritual leader. When Jesus refers to the woman He just healed, He doesn't call her a disabled woman. He calls her "a daughter of Abraham" (v. 16 NIV). There it is. Words of blessing. He doesn't see her as an elderly crippled woman. He sees her as a child of the great patriarch of the Jewish people. Imagine her walking home that day. She's standing up straight for the first time in almost twenty years. She feels ten feet tall. She's seeing things she hasn't seen in years. She's looking people in the eye. And ringing in her ears are the words "daughter of Abraham."

Words Shape Destinies

There's another great example of the power of voice found in the Old Testament character of Joshua. He was the successor to Moses. How intimidating would that be? God has told Moses that he won't lead the nation of Israel into the promised land and that Joshua will be taking his place as the leader of the nation. When speaking of Joshua, the Lord tells Moses, "Encourage him, for he will lead Israel as they take possession of it" (Deut. 1:38).

There it is again. Words of blessing. If you do a study on Joshua's life, you discover that the word *courage* comes up again and again. Joshua hears the words "be strong and courageous" directly from God, from Moses, and even from the people of the nation. Here we find God telling Moses to *encourage* Joshua. The Bible doesn't ever talk about this explicitly, but you just have to wonder if Joshua struggled with fear and self-doubt.

Even though God spoke to Joshua directly, apparently that wasn't sufficient. Sometimes we need the blessing of God in the voice of a human.

I can definitely relate to Joshua. For twenty years I served as a lead pastor and then was asked to join the team at Saddleback Church with Rick Warren. I had pastored small and medium-sized churches, so when I was invited to serve as a pastor at Saddleback, I was ecstatic and terrified all at the same time. I remember having thoughts like these in those days: *I am in way over my head. What if they discover that I'm not who they think I am? What if I can't do this job? What if they conclude I'm a poser? I don't belong here.*

But my boss, Doug Slaybaugh, who was the executive pastor at the time, believed in me. When I didn't have faith in myself, I borrowed some of his faith in me. He spoke confidence and blessing into my life. He didn't just believe in me, he spoke words of "blessing" to me. I will always be grateful.

Sometimes in the course of life, someone will speak a word of blessing that will literally become a defining moment in your journey. I think that is exactly what happened in Deuteronomy 31. Moses speaks blessing into Joshua's life in front of the whole nation. "Then Moses called for Joshua, and as all Israel watched, he said to him, 'Be strong and courageous! . . . Do not be afraid or discouraged, for the LORD will personally go ahead of you. He will be with you; he will neither fail you nor abandon you'" (vv. 7–8). I can only imagine how many times in the coming years that Joshua would go back to that moment and to those words of blessing spoken over him.

In an unexpected moment, I had someone speak a word of blessing to me that became a defining moment. It's a very long story, but after almost seven years at Saddleback, I made the decision to step down from my position as executive pastor. It was certainly one of the hardest things I've ever done. In many ways it had been my dream job, and I thought I could finish out my ministry there. But let's just say I wasn't in a good place and stepped down without having any place to go. On my final day, my assistant pulled together a little farewell gathering in the executive area.

They gave people a chance to share a few words, and everyone was very kind and gracious. But my friend Stevie K. said something that stuck in my spirit. He said, "When I think of Lance, I think of someone who is a pastor to pastors." I didn't give it much thought at the time, but his words of blessing would have a huge impact in my life. A couple months later, through a very clear call from God, I would begin a ministry called Replenish. Replenish focuses on coaching and pastoring leaders.

Before I wrap up this chapter, there is one other moment in the life of Joshua that I want you to see. If we fast-forward to Joshua 10, we find Joshua as the commander of the armies of Israel, who are about to do battle with the Amorite kings who are going to attack Israel's ally, the Gibeonites. These Amorite armies get into position to attack the Gibeonites, and the Gibeonites send a plea for help to Joshua. Joshua and his army ride all night, take the Amorite armies by surprise, and slaughter them.

The five Amorite kings have all hidden in a cave. After the battle, Joshua has them brought out of the cave. He calls his commanders over and, as a symbolic act, has them place their feet on the necks of these foreign kings.

> "Don't ever be afraid or discouraged," Joshua told his men. "Be strong and courageous." (Josh. 10:25)

Do those words sound familiar? The words of blessing that had been spoken over him have now taken root and are bearing fruit in his life. He is now walking out the words that had been spoken over him.

Your mess can become your message.

Joshua has been transformed. His fear, inadequacy, and self-doubt have turned into strength and courage. And now he is able to speak that into the lives of others. The words of blessing spoken over him now become the words of blessing he speaks to others.

When I left Saddleback, I began a journey of emotional health, soul care, and healthy rhythms. My life was transformed, and what had been my mess now has become my message, as I get to pastor other leaders. Thank you, Stevie K., for speaking words of blessing into my life.

So how are you doing at using the gift of voice to speak blessing? What kind of grade would you give yourself? How are you doing at speaking blessing to your team members and those at work? What about speaking blessing to your spouse? Your kids? A good friend? A complete stranger? Let me challenge you to work at consistently making deposits in people's emotional bank accounts through words of blessing.

This week, be sensitive to those subtle promptings. Listen for those whispers from the Spirit. As God leads you, be generous to speak a "word" into people's lives—a word of hope and belief and faith and potential and challenge.

It might just be a moment that changes the trajectory of their life.

REFLECTION/DISCUSSION QUESTIONS

1. When you think back on your childhood, what are some messages that were spoken into your life?

2. Who is one person whose words left a positive mark on your soul? What has been the ripple effect of their words on your life?

3. Where are you most tempted to be negative with your words?

4. How would you rate yourself as an encourager? What could you do to take your encouragement of others to the next level?

24

Take a Moment to Create a Moment

The "occasionally remarkable" moments shouldn't be left to chance! They should be planned for, invested in.

CHIP HEATH

THE BEST THINGS IN LIFE are not things: they are "moments."

There are moments that forever shape a nation. You could probably tell me exactly where you were in 2001 when the 9/11 attack took place. That moment still defines us as a nation.

If you're a sports fan, there are epic moments. *Sports Illustrated* said (and I agree) that the greatest moment in sports history was the 1980 US Olympic Hockey Team in the semifinals against Russia. It was a David-and-Goliath moment in sports.

A ragtag group of college students defeated the legendary Russian Olympic Team that had not lost an Olympic hockey game since 1968. When the Americans went up 4–3 against the Russians, all of America held its breath for those final minutes. It was an unforgettable moment in sports.

In the same way, there are moments that define a life and give it meaning, texture, and richness. Moments can be big or small, dramatic or subtle, joyful or painful; but they are the moments that make us come alive. I don't know about you, but I don't want to punch the time clock of life and sleepwalk through my days. With the one and only life I've been given, I want to experience as many moments as possible.

The Magic of Moments

In his inspiring book *A Million Miles in a Thousand Years*, Donald Miller spoke to Bob Goff, who seems to be a ninja of creating moments: "I asked Bob what was the key to living such a great story. . . . So he thought about it and said he didn't think we should be afraid to embrace whimsy. I asked him what he meant by *whimsy*, and he struggled to define it. He said it's that nagging idea that life could be magical; it could be special if we were only willing to take a few risks."[1]

So let me ask you, what kind of story are you writing with your life these days? Is your heart getting bigger and expanding with love for people? Or is your heart shrinking and shriveling? Are you more alive with wonder and awe than you were last year? When is the last time whimsy made it into your day? Are you soaking up and absorbing moments, or are you always in such a hurry that you blow past the moments that actually make life worth living? What would those closest to you say?

God is the original moment maker. He gave us, as people created in His image, the capacity to experience moments and also to create moments. God didn't create us as machines for a utilitarian purpose, only to be thrown on the scrap heap once we break down. He created us as human beings with emotions and memories. We are hardwired for moments.

For some of us, the baby step we need to take is to actually start enjoying the moments that God sends our way. Sometimes these show up unannounced. In the middle of a normal Tuesday, we get serendipitously blindsided. Right then we get to decide whether we'll slow down long enough to enjoy the moment.

I remember a particular cold day when a moment snuck up on me. We had received several inches of fresh snow at our home in Colorado. We decided this was the perfect time to introduce our granddaughters to sledding. We bundled them up and took them out to the hill at the side of our house. It was a great memory watching my two oldest granddaughters have their first experience with sledding. A day or so later, my daughter-in-law sent me a seven-second video of little Macy coming down the hill on the sled. She was bundled up and looked like the Michelin Man (think big white marshmallow), but you could hear her squeal with delight as she went down the hill. I can't begin to tell you how much joy and delight I had lingering over that seven-second video. I know I watched it dozens of times.

In his book *The Motivation Manifesto*, Brendan Burchard says that awareness can stop time.[2] "Awareness is humanity's best weapon against time. So, let us always remember our capacities to be gifted time benders. We have an extraordinary ability to slow the moment down, to wade into it, to feel it swirl around us." He then ponders what life would be like if we could be present just two beats longer.[3]

So I started wondering what it would look like to take a moment to enjoy a moment.

- ► Instead of gulping down a meal, what if you savored each bite?
- ► Instead of a peck on the cheek, what if you kissed your spouse two seconds longer?
- ► Instead of going on to the next song, what if you lingered over the one you just listened to?
- ► Instead of just reading a few Bible verses and moving on with your day, what if you savored the moment of being with God?
- ► Instead of responding to another email, what if you just took a few moments to delight in your child or grandchild?

▸ Instead of rushing to the next appointment, what if you
took two seconds to whisper a prayer of gratitude for the
life you get to live?

Maybe even more meaningful than experiencing a moment ourselves is creating a moment for others.

The book of Mark records a supper party where a woman barges
in and makes a scene. But her actions that night actually create a
moment that lives on to this day.

While Jesus is having dinner at Simon's house, this uninvited
woman approaches Jesus. She is carrying an expensive bottle of
perfume. She breaks the seal and pours the perfume on Jesus's head.

To better get a sense of the emotion and ethos of this moment,
I want you to read Luke's description. Luke 7:38 says, "Then she
knelt behind him at his feet, weeping. Her tears fell on his feet,
and she wiped them off with her hair. Then she kept kissing his
feet and putting perfume on them."

Can you sense the emotion of this scene? This is a moment.
It's a breach of social custom and etiquette for this woman to
enter the house of a Pharisee. But she bursts into the room with a
spontaneous, awkward, unrestrained, uninhibited, lavish, exces-
sive expression of love.

I love the impulsiveness and spontaneity of this scene. In a way,
she gives what we all want. We all like being surprised by gestures
of love. We love a surprise party or a kidnap breakfast with friends.
And we have all felt the urge to do something lavish and "over the
top" for someone we love. But more times than not we push the
urge back down, talk ourselves out of it, choose to play it safe,
and get on with our to-do list. We miss the chance to watch people
light up because we took the risk to create a moment.

Interestingly, Jesus says she has done a *good* thing: not a careless thing, not an irresponsible thing, not a wasteful thing. She has
done a good thing in seizing *this* moment to create a moment. She
will not have this opportunity again.

Then Jesus says *she has done what she could.* You can't ask for
anything more. She did what she could with what she had. She

didn't know that Jesus was about to be crucified. But she saw an opportunity to express her devotion and she grabbed it. And now her story lives on thousands of years later.

Crafting a Moment

Sometimes moments happen because we spontaneously do something uncommon and out of the box. But it is also possible to plan a moment. We can be the architect and author of a moment.

Like my friend Julie Mullins says, "Expectation requires preparation."[4]

If you're an expectant mom, you're preparing your life and home for the arrival of that little infant. You're purchasing a car seat and a crib and diapers. If you're a couple expecting to get married in the next few months, you're preparing to make that moment as special and meaningful as possible.

Next week Connie and I are hosting our annual cousin camp for our four granddaughters. We have been planning for this for many weeks. We have a plan for each day. The goal is not to just keep them busy and occupied each day but rather to create moments that will be a lifelong memory. We don't want cousin camp to just be tolerable, we want it to be treasurable.

Here's the point. Often, moments happen because someone took the time and effort to look ahead and create the right environment. You have to take a moment to create a moment.

If you want to be a world-class moment maker, you have to really pay attention. You must have your "notice" antenna finely tuned.

In his book *Excellence Wins*, Horst Schulze tells of a housekeeper at a Ritz Carlton who was paying attention. One day when emptying the trash, she noticed the guest had picked out the nuts from the chocolate chip cookies. So, she told the chef and he made a special tray of cookies (without nuts) and had them waiting in the guest's room when he returned that evening.[5]

I remember when we were living in California and I took my car in to get a minor repair done. While I waited, the lady at the service counter asked me if I would like something to drink. I told her I would love a Diet Coke. A few months later, I had to take my car in again for repair. When I checked in my car, that same receptionist had a cold Diet Coke sitting on the counter waiting for me. Her thoughtfulness to make a note in my record the last time I had come in created a small, but awesome, moment.

Go for It

I just wonder how many times this past week we missed an opportunity to surprise someone with love and create a treasured moment. We live in a world that is driven to achieve, so we obsess on efficiency and productivity. This hard-driving, bottom-line lifestyle often mitigates against spontaneous, extravagant acts that create moments. And with each time we push the urge back down, our hearts shrink and shrivel just a little more.

I am a fan of good stewardship. That's a nice way of saying I can be frugal and tight. But there is a time and place for lavish expressions of love and generosity. We rarely create moments by being practical and frugal. It makes me think of being in a small group meeting one night. As an icebreaker, I asked people to share about the worst Christmas gift they had ever received. One of the ladies in the group looked over at her husband, grinned, and then proceeded to tell us about a gift she had received from him a couple years earlier. She shared that when she opened the gift, she was confused and didn't even know what it was. He had to explain to her that it was an insulation blanket for their water heater. *Ouch.* An insulation blanket is highly practical. But it will never create a moment—at least not a positive moment.

Many years ago now, an unexpected moment took place during a Sunday morning service. We had decided to reach out to the college campus located down the street from the church. We helped students move into the dorms and in the process invited them to visit our church.

A week or two later, we were well into our worship service (in fact, I had already started my sermon) when a college student walked in the back door. He was wearing tattered jeans and a T-shirt. He was scanning the room looking for a place to sit, trying not to disturb the service. No one moved to help or offer him a seat. Finally, he simply made his way down the aisle a few feet and plopped down on the floor in the middle of the aisle.

I wasn't quite sure what to do, so I just kept preaching. Finally, after a couple minutes one of the older leaders in our church got up. I'm sure some in the congregation thought, *Finally! It's about time someone in leadership went and told the young man that this is inappropriate for a worship service.* Without saying a word, this older church member sat on the floor with the young man and stayed there through the rest of the sermon.

I love stories like that because they are about an unexpected moment. The best moments come from hearts overflowing with love and grace. To create moments like this, you are going to have to be impractical at times.

Listen, my friend: you really don't know what lies ahead or how long you'll be here. You have today. You have right now. You have one life. You have this moment. You can't do everything. You can't meet every need. You can't bless every person. But you can capture and create moments. Do what you can.

To create moments, you must break the script, go off-road, and color outside the lines. I want to close this chapter by challenging you to seize the moment to create a moment. I'm convinced that every week, we have multiple opportunities to create a moment or to linger over a moment.

Put down the insulation blanket, and pick up the bottle of perfume.

REFLECTION/DISCUSSION QUESTIONS

1. Share a time when someone blessed you with an unexpected moment.

2. Describe a time in the recent past when you were in awe of something.

3. If you had been a dinner guest that night when the uninvited woman came and poured perfume over the head of Jesus, how would you have felt during that moment?

4. What crazy, out-of-the-box, impractical, lavish way can you create a moment for someone? Share your idea and come up with a plan to pull it off. You'll be glad you did.

CHAPTER 25

~~What~~ Who Will Be Your Legacy?

A righteous person is one who lives
for the next generation.

DIETRICH BONHOEFFER.

I HAVE A QUESTION for you to ponder. Outside of Jesus, what has most positively shaped and influenced your life? Seriously. Take a moment to ponder that question. My suspicion is that your answer isn't a song, a seminar, or a sermon. It probably wasn't a "what," it was likely a "who." I feel confident it was a "someone." It was a person; a person who took an interest in you and invested in you. You got to benefit from their wisdom and experiences. You listened to their stories. You got to watch their life up close and personal. And they left an indelible imprint on your one and only life. I am now in my early sixties, and I'm fully aware that I have more life in the rearview mirror than in the windshield. With each passing decade, I can hear the tick of the clock get louder as my life winds down. I spend way more time these days pondering the word *legacy*. What will I leave behind? What can I give that will outlast me?

It was never God's plan that you or I would slink onto the stage of history, mundanely live out our days, and quietly exit without making a contribution that impacts life both here and in eternity. As I get older, I have a growing conviction that my greatest legacy will be the handful of lives that I loved and invested in deeply.

Many years ago, a friend who led a parachurch ministry shared a principle that guided his approach to ministry: more time spent with fewer people equals greater impact. Those nine words have taken root in my soul. To really live the life you long to live, I believe you have to figure out who are the few you will pour your life into. If you have children or grandchildren, they should certainly be at the top of the list. But perhaps there's someone at work or at your gym or in your church or in your neighborhood who would be a good candidate for you to invest in. An old proverb says, "In one apple there are a few seeds, but in one seed, there are thousands of apples." As you invest in and influence one life, the potential multiplication of your investment is staggering.

I love the call and challenge of Psalm 78:4–6:

> We will not hide these truths from our children;
> 　　we will tell the next generation
> about the glorious deeds of the LORD,
> 　　about his power and his mighty wonders.
> For he issued his laws to Jacob;
> 　　he gave his instructions to Israel.
> He commanded our ancestors
> 　　to teach them to their children,
> so the next generation might know them—
> 　　even the children not yet born—
> 　　and they in turn will teach their own children.

It is definitely on my radar to make sure my grandkids know about the glorious deeds of the Lord. We have a mountain property, and when I'm there with my granddaughters, we usually try to take a hike up the mountain. Up the hill is a bit of a flat spot, and a couple of years ago when we hiked to that spot, I talked to them about memorials in the Bible. I shared with them that memorials were to serve as a constant reminder of what God had done in the past. So that day we each gathered a few rocks and made a memorial as a reminder of what God had done for us. Now each time we're at the cabin, the kids want to hike up to the memorial. Every time we go, I tell them another Bible story of something great God has done, and then we each add a rock to the memorial. My hope and prayer are that these little seeds of investment in them will take root in their lives, and someday they will in turn teach their children about the power and mighty wonders of God.

The Impact of Investment

As I think back over my life, I'm filled with gratitude for the people who took the time to invest in me. I never officially had a mentor, but a number of people have profoundly shaped my life just by their interest in me and giving me access to their world.

Early on in my journey, there was a guy named Rocky Freeman who came to speak at our church. God used him to spark a true spiritual renewal in our church that had impact for years to come. My parents, who have tremendous gifts of hospitality, would always invite visiting preachers to come to our home. I remember several times when Rocky would sit at our kitchen table talking about God and the Bible. The conversations would sometimes last for hours, and my dad would let me stay up late into the night listening to those conversations.

Then, after I married and was in Bible college, Rocky and his wife, Pat, would invite us to come and spend time with them at their home. We were poor students, so all we had to do was get there and they took care of everything else. They had a great pool in their backyard, and we would spend hours swimming, talking, hanging out, and grilling. There was no fanfare or elaborate plans or expensive restaurants. They simply loved on us and gave us the ministry of "presence." And it profoundly impacted our marriage and ministry.

In more recent years, my life has been impacted by my friendship with Pete Scazzero. For several years, Pete was an indirect mentor through his writings. Then, a few years ago, I had the opportunity to get acquainted with Pete and his wife, Geri. I immediately had a great connection with them, and since then Pete and I have been spending some time together.

Last year when Pete and I got together again in New York, he had planned a walking tasting tour through Queens. The food was great, but the conversation was even better. Just like my times with Rocky Freeman over three decades ago, there wasn't anything elaborate or formal in my time with Pete. The secret sauce was unhurried time and access to them and their world.

More Caught Than Taught

I really do believe that the Christian life is more caught than taught.

This certainly was the approach Jesus took. He didn't offer the disciples a Bible class or simply hand them a big binder full of notes. He recruited twelve very ordinary men and over the course of three years did life with them and poured His life into them. Up close and personal. He gave them access. There is power in proximity.

After three years of life together, Jesus ascended back into heaven and entrusted the future of His kingdom into their hands. His primary strategy was one of reproducing kingdom life in those twelve men by doing life with them. You will never do anything more Christlike in all your life than investing in the lives of others.

I love that one of the names of Jesus is Immanuel, which literally translated means "God with us." He came incarnationally. He didn't choose to come virtually. He didn't opt for a podcast or webinar to reveal Himself. He came in the flesh and did life "with" the disciples.

This theme of personal investment and multiplication runs all the way through the Bible. In 2 Timothy 2:2, Paul writes to his young protégé, "You have heard me teach things that have been confirmed by many reliable witnesses. Now teach these truths to other trustworthy people who will be able to pass them on to others."

The word *teach* (sometimes translated *entrust*) is a banker's term. It literally means "to deposit." When you make a deposit into your savings account, you're going to draw interest. It's an investment because it brings a return. The same is true when you take an interest in someone and invest in them.

Paul would also say, "For even if you had ten thousand others to teach you about Christ, you have only one spiritual father. For I became your father in Christ Jesus when I preached the Good News to you. So I urge you to imitate me" (1 Cor. 4:15–16).

Becoming a "spiritual father" might sound intimidating. But it doesn't have to be. What Paul is communicating is that we need more than truth and instruction. We need relationship. We need proximity. We need access. We need an example to follow. This is also Paul's heartbeat in 1 Thessalonians 2:8: "We loved you so much, we were delighted to share with you not only the gospel of God, but our lives as well" (NIV). That passage drips with personal investment.

Tips for Pouring into Somebody

Hopefully you are convinced that pouring into somebody in your sphere of influence is a worthwhile investment. I know your life is full and busy, so I want to share some practical strategies to help this be doable and enjoyable. Healthy relationships are a joy and are life-giving, not life-sucking.

Employ the "As You Go" Principle

Deuteronomy 6 was the first passage memorized by Jewish boys and girls. This passage is called the Shema and is a declaration that there is but one true God; it also contains a challenge to love God with everything that is in you. Right after the Shema, we read, "And you must commit yourselves wholeheartedly to these commands that I am giving you today" (v. 6). Verses 7–9 describe how they would infuse God's truth into their hearts. Moses said, "Repeat them again and again to your children. Talk about them when you are at home and when you are on the road, when you are going to bed and when you are getting up. Tie them to your hands and wear them on your forehead as reminders. Write them on the doorposts of your house and on your gates."

In other words, use everyday experiences as teachable moments.

As you think about investing in someone, here is a good question to ask: "What am I already planning to do to which I could invite someone to join me?" You don't need an outline or a study guide. You're simply giving them access and proximity. And that is a gift.

Your Life Is the Curriculum

As I teach people about investing in others, I often get a stiff-arm from them. I hear statements like, "I wouldn't know what to teach them. I don't have anything to offer." You absolutely have something to offer: YOU! Your life is the curriculum, and you are an expert when it comes to your life. You can share what you've learned, how you're navigating a situation at work or with one of your kids, mistakes you've made, or stories of God's faithfulness.

> O God, you have taught me from my earliest childhood,
> and I constantly tell others about the wonderful things
> you do.
> Now that I am old and gray,
> do not abandon me, O God.
> Let me proclaim your power to this new generation,
> your mighty miracles to all who come after me. (Ps.
> 71:17–18)

Just like the psalmist, from your early childhood you've been learning life lessons that can be passed on to others.

My wife actually wrote a book on lifestyle mentoring. And she wanted me to be sure to mention that she was the first published author in the family. In her book, Connie says, "Mentoring is a lifestyle, not a program. It is basically taking the relationships God has put in your life, recognizing the God moments, and intentionally sharing what God has taught you in those moments and circumstances."[1]

Challenge and Care

When you invest in someone, there needs to be a balance of personal care and intentional challenge. Paul demonstrated this balance in his words from 1 Thessalonians 2:11–12:

> For you know that we dealt with each of you as a father deals with his own children, encouraging, comforting and urging you to live lives worthy of God, who calls you into his kingdom and glory. (NIV)

Good fathers encourage and comfort. They care. They speak life-giving words to us. But good fathers also urge, which is the idea of challenging, exhorting, and imploring. When we invest in people, we don't just care for them, we also help them get better. We help them grow. We stretch them.

The best coaches I have had in my life believed in me and cheered me on. But they also pushed me and stretched me to do things I would have never done on my own.

Moments, Seasons, and Lifetime

This is also a principle I learned from Connie. Sometimes the idea of investing in people can feel daunting. It helps to realize there are different levels of investment. Sometimes you'll invest in someone through a brief onetime conversation. The key here is to be on the lookout for those "God moments" that intersect your path.

There are also people whom you'll invest in for a season. Earlier I mentioned Rocky Freeman and the investment he and his wife made in us. It didn't last forever. It was for a season, but that season had a huge influence on my life and future.

And then there might be that person or two you have such a special connection with that your investment in them will become a lifelong relationship.

There's a moment in the Bible when the apostle Paul is talking about Jesus coming again. He asks an interesting question as he thinks about the return of Jesus: What will be our hope, our joy, our crown? In other words, Paul asks, "What would I be most proud of and what would I be most excited to show Jesus?" I love his answer. "Is it not you? Indeed, you are our glory and joy" (1 Thess. 2:19–20 NIV).

Paul recognizes that the ultimate legacy he will leave behind will not be an inventory of possessions but an investment in people. So this week, look for a moment when you can invest in someone. Who knows? That moment could turn into a season or even a lifetime relationship.

REFLECTION/DISCUSSION QUESTIONS

1. Who is someone who significantly shaped your life? What specific ways did they invest in you that made such an impact?

2. When you think about investing in someone younger, how does that feel?

3. What is something you do regularly where you could employ the "as you go" principle?

4. Who is someone you could imagine investing in? What would that look like, and is there a next step you could take with them?

Conclusion

I SPENT A GOOD bit of time really praying through and thinking through what I would want to say in this conclusion. The first thing I want to say to you is . . . thanks for staying with this to the end of the book. I'm impressed, and maybe a little surprised. I know how easy it is to put a book down and never make it to the end. I sincerely hope it has encouraged, challenged, and helped you.

As we come to the end of the book, I want to challenge you to create what I call a Life Manifesto. A Life Purpose Statement is about the "why" and "what" of my life. A Life Manifesto is a little more about the "how" of my life. It begins to define how I will live out my Life Purpose. It might be helpful to think of a Life Manifesto like a trellis. A trellis is a structure or framework on which a vine can grow. A Life Manifesto is the framework on which to grow a beautiful life.

Right after this conclusion is an exercise to create your own personal Life Manifesto. I have also included a copy of my Life Manifesto. It's something that I come back to over and over. It keeps me centered. It reminds me of my priorities. It helps me course correct. And it points me to the kind of life I want to live. Please consider taking the time to craft yours.

Here are a couple final thoughts for you to consider. At the end of the day, the quality and richness of your life are inextricably connected to your willingness and ability to lead yourself. Leading yourself well will be the most courageous undertaking of your life. It's so easy to drift. It's so easy to fall into faulty thinking. It's so easy to let the voices around you push you off course. It's so easy to get distracted. But staying true to God's purposes and true to yourself and what really matters to you, that's a tall order.

I believe there are a ton of practical ideas in these chapters that you could implement and steps you could take that would help you live a better life. And I genuinely hope that happens.

But I have a deeper longing. And I've lived long enough to have realistic expectations about the impact a book can have. My deepest longing is that a few people who read this book will change the trajectory of their lives. Like the prodigal son, they'll have a moment when they "come to themselves." They'll have a moment of holy discontent with how they've been living. They'll have a moment of sobering clarity about God's purpose for their lives. They'll have a moment of accessing their deepest longings. They'll have a moment of fierce courage.

You get only one shot at this life.

The clock is ticking.

Life Manifesto

THE WORDS *LIFE MANIFESTO* can sound daunting and intimidating. Creating your own Life Manifesto should be fun and engaging. It is simply you putting into words what matters to you and how you want to live your one life. For me, this has been a document that took quite some time to think through and create. And over the last few years, I've changed a couple statements and added a couple. So don't rush this exercise. Let it have some breathing room.

By way of example, I have inserted my Life Manifesto. This is something I try to revisit pretty regularly (at least quarterly) to assess how I'm doing at actually living out these statements.

I've provided some space for you to at least get started in drafting a Life Manifesto. I encourage you to start writing out some phrases or statements that begin to define how you want to go about living out your Life Purpose Statement (see page 65–66).

I would also encourage you to run your thoughts by someone who knows you really well and will speak honestly into your life. Sometimes other people can see things that we value more clearly and objectively than we can.

I'm glad that several years ago I took the time to articulate my Life Manifesto. It has served me well and is the trellis upon which I am trying to build a rich and beautiful life.

Lance's Life Manifesto

- I will meet with God each day before I meet with people.
- Connie will be my best friend, and I will be her biggest cheerleader.
- I will be present with people and with God . . . this requires "slow" and "space."
- I will pursue a healthy rhythm of life and relentlessly practice Sabbath.
- I will pray faith-filled prayers.
- I will make much of Jesus and not make much of myself.
- I will discipline myself to regularly unplug from technology.
- I will embrace both truth and grace in every relationship.
- I will be an available grandfather and dad and intentionally invest in the spiritual development of my family.
- I will have people in my life who can rebuke me . . . and who love me enough to protect me from myself.
- I will wisely and tenaciously manage my time and health. I've only got one life and one body.
- I will honor and love people and speak blessing into their lives.
- I will intentionally pursue a handful of lifelong and life-giving friendships.
- I will enjoy the beauty of nature—it refreshes my soul.
- I will live simply and give generously.

Life Manifesto Draft

Notes

Introduction

1. Michael Yankoski, *The Sacred Year: Mapping the Soulscape of Spiritual Practice—How Contemplating Apples, Living in a Cave, and Befriending a Dying Woman Revived My Life* (Nashville: W Publishing, 2014), 112.

Chapter 1 It's Later Than It's Ever Been

1. See Julia Keller, "The Mysterious Ambrose Redmoon's Healing Words," *Chicago Tribune*, March 29, 2002, https://www.chicagotribune.com/news/ct-xpm-2002-03-29-0203290018-story.html.

Chapter 2 Wherever You Go, There You Are

1. Dr. Henry Cloud and Dr. John Townsend, *It's Not My Fault: The No-Excuse Plan for Overcoming Life's Obstacles* (Nashville: Thomas Nelson, 2007), 25.

2. Quoted in John Maxwell, *Today Matters: 12 Daily Practices to Guarantee Tomorrow's Success* (New York: Center Street Hachette Book Group, 2004), 21.

3. Brendon Burchard, *The Motivation Manifesto: 9 Declarations to Claim Your Personal Power* (Carlsbad, CA: Hay House, Inc., 2014), xii.

4. François Fénelon, *The Seeking Heart* (Jacksonville, FL: SeedSowers, 1992), 147.

5. Benjamin Franklin, QuoteInvestigator.com, https://quoteinvestigator.com/2018/03/08/excuses/.

Chapter 3 Plan, but Don't Presume

1. Vocabulary.com, s.v. "presumption," accessed February 9, 2021, https://www.vocabulary.com/dictionary/presumption.

Chapter 4 The Most Important Word in the Bible

1. Rick Warren, *The Purpose Driven Life* (Grand Rapids: Zondervan, 2002), 18.
2. Warren, *Purpose Driven Life*, 17.

3. Wikipedia, s.v. "glory (religion)," last modified January 14, 2021, https://en.wikipedia.org/wiki/Glory_(religion).

Chapter 5 Begin at the End

1. Yankoski, *Sacred Year*, 105.
2. Yankoski, *Sacred Year*, 105.
3. Dan Miller and Jared Angaza, *Wisdom Meets Passion: When Generations Collide and Collaborate* (Nashville: Thomas Nelson, 2012), 134.
4. Stephen R. Covey, *First Things First* (New York: Simon & Schuster, 1994), 19.
5. Oscar Wilde, *DeProfundis* (letter published in 1905).

Chapter 6 Are Souls Overrated?

1. *Bedazzled*, directed by Harold Ramis (Los Angeles: 20th Century Fox, 2000), DVD.
2. Quoted in John Ortberg, *Soul Keeping: Caring for the Most Important Part of You* (Grand Rapids: Zondervan, 2014), 39.
3. Quoted in Ortberg, *Soul Keeping*, 11.
4. Leighton Ford, *The Attentive Life: Discerning God's Presence in All Things* (Downers Grove, IL: InterVarsity, 2008), 11.

Chapter 7 What Story Are You Telling Yourself?

1. E. E. Cummings, "A Poet's Advice to Students" in *A Miscellany Revised*, ed. George James Firmage (New York: October House, 1965), 335.
2. "The Scar Study," Adventist Youth Society, accessed February 26, 2021, https://youthays.wordpress.com/a-z-illustration/the-scar-study/.
3. Judith Hougen, *Transformed into Fire: Discovering Your True Identity as God's Beloved* (Grand Rapids: Kregel, 2002), 65.
4. Adapted from David Benner, *The Gift of Being Yourself: The Sacred Call to Self-Discovery* (Downers Grove, IL: InterVarsity, 2004), 92.
5. Alicia Britt Chole, *Anonymous: Jesus' Hidden Years . . . and Yours* (Nashville: Thomas Nelson, 2006), 41.
6. Henri Nouwen, *The Life of the Beloved: Spiritual Living in a Secular World* (New York: Crossroads Publishing, 1992), 106.

Chapter 8 Is Self-Care Selfish?

1. Geri Scazzero with Pete Scazzero, *I Quit: Stop Pretending Everything Is Fine and Change Your Life* (Grand Rapids: Zondervan, 2010), 66.

Chapter 9 Techno-Soul

1. Joel Shannon, "Teen Broke into Home, Woke the Owners and Asked to Use Their Wi-Fi, California Police Say," *USA Today*, July 27, 2018, https://www.usatoday.com/story/news/nation-now/2018/07/27/teen-burglar-woke-couple-ask-wi-fi-california-police-say/853352002/.
2. Ray Kurzweil, "The Law of Accelerating Returns," Kurzweil Accelerating Intelligence, March 7, 2001, https://www.kurzweilai.net/the-law-of-accelerating-returns.

3. Cal Newport, *Digital Minimalism: Choosing a Focused Life in a Noisy World* (New York: Portfolio/Penguin, 2018), 5.

4. Newport, *Digital Minimalism*, 104.

5. Notes on "I Used to Be a Human Being by Andrew Sullivan," Nateliason.com, accessed February 26, 2021, https://www.nateliason.com/notes/i-used-to-be-a-human-being-andrew-sullivan.

6. Newport, *Digital Minimalism*, 108.

7. Marshall McLuhan, *Understanding Media: The Extension of Man* (New York: McGraw Hill, 1964), 1.

8. Neil Postman, *Technopoly: The Surrender of Culture to Technology* (New York: Random House, 1992), 18.

9. Marshall McLuhan and Lewis L. Lapham, *Understanding Media: The Extensions of Man* (Cambridge, MA: Massachusetts Institute of Technology, 1994), xi.

10. Newport, *Digital Minimalism*, xiii.

11. Tristan Harris, "How a Handful of Companies Control Billions of Minds Every Day," TED video, April 2017, https://www.ted.com/talks/tristan_harris_how_a_handful_of_tech_companies_control_billions_of_minds_every_day?language=en.

12. John Mark Comer, *The Ruthless Elimination of Hurry: How to Stay Emotionally Healthy and Spiritually Alive in the Chaos of the Modern World* (Colorado Springs: WaterBrook, 2019), 39.

13. Nicholas Carr, *The Shallows: What the Internet Is Doing to Our Brains* (New York: W. W. Norton, 2011), 114.

14. Sherry Turkle, *Reclaiming Conversation: The Power of Talk in a Digital Age* (New York: Penguin, 2015), 3.

15. Christi Straub, "What My iPhone Stole from Me," Famous at Home, June 25, 2014, https://www.joshuastraub.com/2014/06/25/what-my-iphone-stole-from-me/.

Chapter 10 You Owe Me

1. Charles C. W. Cooke, "OWS Protester Wants College Paid for Because That Is What He Wants," *National Review*, October 12, 2011, https://www.nationalreview.com/corner/ows-protester-wants-college-paid-because-what-he-wants-charles-c-w-cooke/.

2. Dr. John Townsend, *The Entitlement Cure: Finding Success in Doing Hard Things the Right Way* (Grand Rapids: Zondervan, 2015), 19.

3. *Cambridge Dictionary*, s.v. "entitlement," accessed January 27, 2021, https://dictionary.cambridge.org/us/dictionary/english/entitlement.

Chapter 11 What's the Big Hurry?

1. Burchard, *Motivation Manifesto*, xvii.

2. Comer, *Ruthless Elimination of Hurry*, 23.

3. Alan Fadling, *An Unhurried Life: Following Jesus' Rhythms of Work and Rest* (Downers Grove, IL: InterVarsity, 2013), 14.

4. Quoted in Fadling, *Unhurried Life*, 9.

5. Anne Lamott (@AnneLamottQuote), "'No' is a complete sentence. It's given me this tremendous sense of power. I'm a little bit drunk on it," Twitter, October 18, 2017, 10:27 a.m., https://twitter.com/AnneLamottQuote/status/920657616707182592.

Chapter 12 Simplicity Isn't So Simple

1. Thomas R. Kelly, *A Testament of Devotion* (New York: Harper & Brothers, 1941), 92.

2. Mindy Caliguire, *Simplicity* (Downers Grove, IL: InterVarsity, 2008), 19.

3. Hans Hofmann Quote, last accessed February 9, 2021, https://www.goodreads.com/quotes/70138-the-ability-to-simplify-means-to-eliminate-the-unnecessary-so.

4. Eugene O'Kelly, *Chasing Daylight: How My Forthcoming Death Transformed My Life* (New York: McGraw Hill, 2008), 14.

5. Quoted in Edward G. Dobson, *Simplicity: Finding Order, Freedom, and Fulfillment for Your Life* (Grand Rapids: Zondervan, 1995), 29.

6. Tish Harrison Warren and Andy Crouch, *Liturgy of the Ordinary: Sacred Practices in Everyday Life* (Downers Grove, IL: InterVarsity, 2016), 33.

7. Dave Hollis (@MrDaveHollis), "In the rush to return to normal, let's use this time to consider what parts of normal are worth rushing back to," Twitter, April 1, 2020, 10:45 a.m., https://twitter.com/mrdavehollis/status/1245361542985637894?lang=en.

8. Paul Borthwick, *Simplify: 106 Ways to Uncomplicate Your Life* (Colorado Springs: Authentic Publishing, 2007), 95.

Chapter 13 The Discipline of the Daily

1. Annie Dillard, *The Writing Life* (New York: Harper & Row, 1989), 32.

2. Tish Harrison Warren, "Courage in the Ordinary," *The Well*, April 3, 2013, https://thewell.intervarsity.org/blog/courage-ordinary.

3. Friedrich Nietzsche, *Beyond Good and Evil* (Hoboken, NJ: Wiley, 2020), 95.

4. Admiral William H. McRaven, "University of Texas at Austin 2014 Commencement Address," University of Texas at Austin, May 19, 2014, YouTube video, https://www.youtube.com/watch?v=pxBQLFLei70.

5. Warren and Crouch, *Liturgy of the Ordinary*, 21.

6. James Clear, *Atomic Habits* (New York: Avery, 2018), 15.

7. Clear, *Atomic Habits*, 7.

8. Clear, *Atomic Habits*, 72.

9. Clear, *Atomic Habits*, 76–77.

Chapter 14 The Divine Rhythm of Life

1. Newport, *Digital Minimalism*, x.

2. Comer, *Ruthless Elimination of Hurry*, 121.

3. Matthew Walker, *Why We Sleep: Unlocking the Power of Sleep and Dreams* (New York: Scribner, 2017), 55.

4. Mark Buchanan, *The Rest of God: Restoring Your Soul by Restoring Sabbath* (Nashville: W Publishing, 2006), 88.

5. Lynne M. Baab, *Sabbath Keeping: Finding Freedom in the Rhythms of Life* (Downers Grove, IL: InterVarsity, 2005), 112.

6. Kevin DeYoung, *Crazy Busy: A (Mercifully) Short Book about a (Really) Big Problem* (Wheaton: Crossway, 2013), 91.

7. Abraham Heschel, *I Asked for Wonder: A Spiritual Anthology* (New York: Crossroad, 1996), 34.

Chapter 15 The Best Day of the Week

1. Dan B. Allender, *Sabbath: The Ancient Practices* (Nashville: Thomas Nelson, 2009), 63.

2. Baab, *Sabbath Keeping*, 35.

3. Buchanan, *Rest of God*, 203.

4. Comer, *Ruthless Elimination of Hurry*, 31.

5. Buchanan, *Rest of God*, 62.

6. Buchanan, *Rest of God*, 129.

7. Clear, *Atomic Habits*, 27.

Chapter 16 The Art of Hanging Out

1. Ruth Haley Barton, "What We Believe about Spiritual Transformation," Transforming Center, 2011, https://transformingcenter.org/2011/01/what-we-believe-about-spiritual-transformation/.

2. A. W. Tozer, *The Pursuit of God* (Camp Hill, PA: Christian Publications, 1993), 15.

3. Quoted in Ortberg, *Soul Keeping*, 20.

4. Quoted in Kyle C. Strobel, *Formed for the Glory of God* (Downers Grove, IL: InterVarsity, 2013), 58.

Chapter 17 Practice Makes Progress

1. Marjorie J. Thompson, *Soul Feast: An Invitation to the Christian Spiritual Life* (Louisville: Westminster John Knox, 1995), 10.

2. Gary L. Thomas, *Seeking the Face of God: The Path to a More Intimate Relationship* (Eugene, OR: Harvest House, 1994), 40.

3. Clear, *Atomic Habits*, 7.

4. Clear, *Atomic Habits*, 251.

5. Clear, *Atomic Habits*, 72.

6. Mindy Caliguire, *Discovering Soul Care* (Downers Grove, IL: InterVarsity, 2007), 81–83.

Chapter 18 The Rotting Tree Syndrome

1. Michael Oh, "The Danger of 'Fruitfulness' without Purity," *Reflection*, August 17, 2017, https://www.mtw.org/stories/details/the-danger-of-fruitfulness-without-purity.

2. Bible Hub, s.v. "hagios," accessed March 1, 2021, https://biblehub.com/greek/40.htm.

3. Quoted in William G. Britton, *Wisdom from the Margins: Daily Readings* (Searcy, AR: Resource Publications, 2018), 7.

Chapter 19 When Losing Can Mean Winning

1. "Americans Defeat the British at Yorktown," History.com, November 24, 2009, https://www.history.com/this-day-in-history/victory-at-yorktown.

2. Martin Luther, *Concordia: The Lutheran Confessions*, 2nd ed. (St. Louis: Concordia Publishing House, 2006), 359.

3. Chip Ingram, *True Spirituality: Becoming a Romans 12 Christian* (New York: Howard Books, 2009), 43–44.

Chapter 20 Surviving Unhappy Endings

1. "2001 Roni and Baby Charity Bowers Die in Plane Shot Down in Peru," This Date in History, accessed February 9, 2021, http://www.safran-arts.com/42day /history/h4apr/20bowers/20bowers.html.

2. Harold Kushner, *When Bad Things Happen to Good People* (New York: Anchor, 2004), 50.

3. Quoted in Philip Yancey, *Disappointment with God: Three Questions No One Asks Aloud* (Grand Rapids: Zondervan, 2004), 200.

4. Yancey, *Disappointment*, 275.

5. "Remembering and Celebrating an Exceptional Life," accessed February 9, 2021, http://sermons.rvbc.cc/ResourceLibrary/Bowers/Bowers.htm.

Chapter 21 The Value of Adding Value

1. Brother Lawrence, *The Practice of the Presence of God* (New Kensington, PA: Whitaker House, 1982).

2. Lexico, s.v. "dignity," accessed February 10, 2021, https://www.lexico.com /en/definition/dignity.

Chapter 23 The Power of a Word

1. "Voice Acoustics: An Introduction," Physclips, UNSW School of Physics, Sydney, Australia, https://www.animations.physics.unsw.edu.au/jw/voice.html.

Chapter 24 Take a Moment to Create a Moment

1. Donald Miller, *A Million Miles in a Thousand Years: What I Learned While Editing My Life* (Nashville: Thomas Nelson, 2009), 167.

2. Burchard, *Motivation Manifesto*, 227.

3. Burchard, *Motivation Manifesto*, 229.

4. Julie Mullins from her conference talk at Christ Fellowship, February 2020.

5. Horst Schulze, *Excellence Wins: A No-Nonsense Guide to Becoming the Best in a World of Compromise* (Grand Rapids: Zondervan, 2019), 40.

Chapter 25 ~~What~~ Who Will Be Your Legacy?

1. Connie Witt and Cathi Workman, *That Makes Two of Us: Lifestyle Mentoring for Women* (Loveland, CO: Group Publishing, 2009), 44.

Lance Witt is the founder of Replenish ministries, the author of *Replenish* and *High-Impact Teams*, and is often referred to as a pastor's pastor. Before launching Replenish, Lance served twenty years as a senior pastor and six years as an executive and teaching pastor at Saddleback Church. For the last fifteen years, Lance has helped people "live and lead from a healthy soul." Lance and his wife, Connie, live in Colorado and have two grown children and four granddaughters. Lance loves fly-fishing, hiking, playing with his grandkids, and New Mexico–style enchiladas.

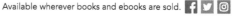

LANCE WITT: A PASTOR TO LEADERS

Head to **REPLENISH.NET** for resources, blogs, and podcasts or to get in contact with Lance.

ALSO FOLLOW HIM ON SOCIAL MEDIA:

 Lance Witt

 Lance_Witt

Connect with

BakerBooks
Relevant. Intelligent. Engaging.

Sign up for announcements about
new and upcoming titles at

BakerBooks.com/SignUp

@ReadBakerBooks